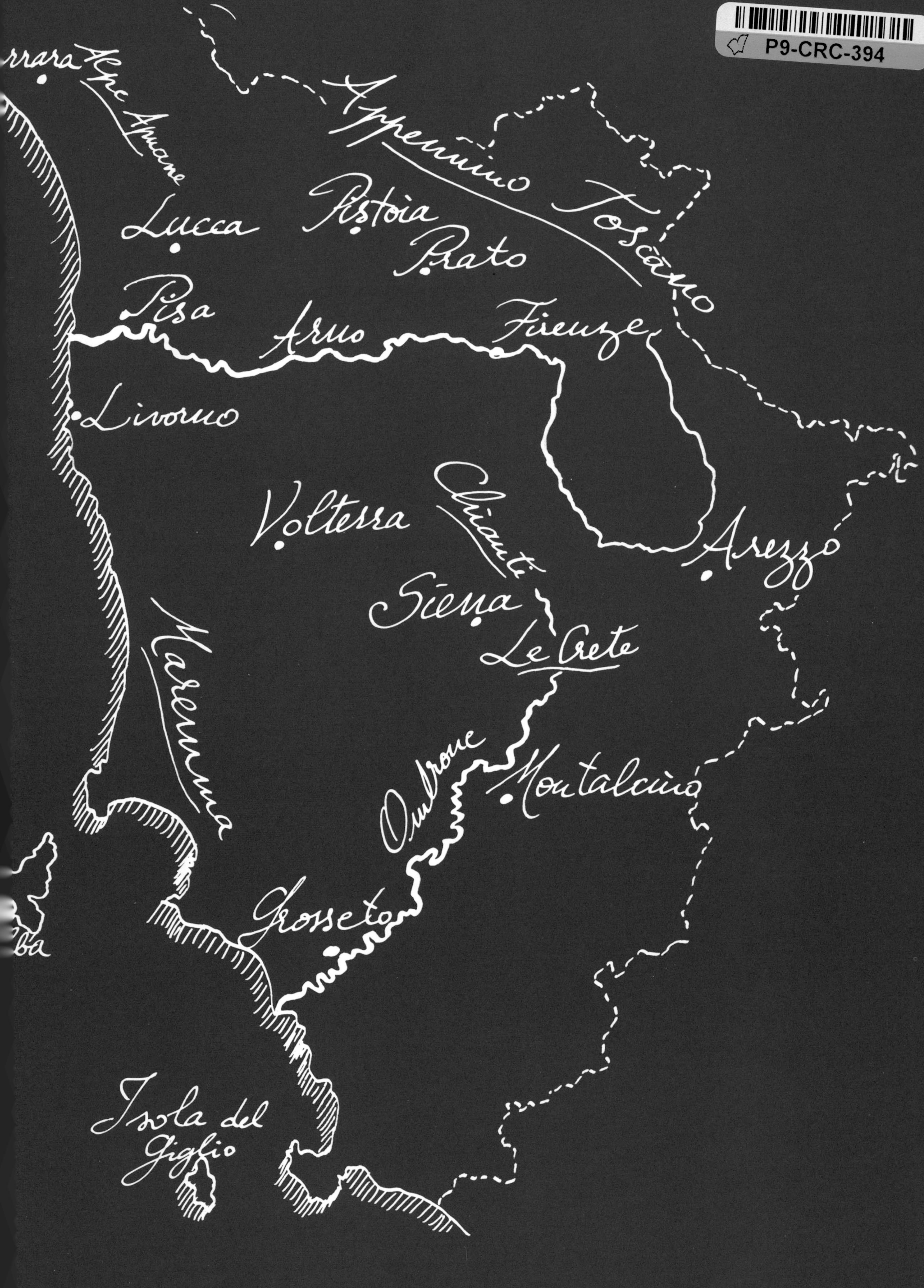

Carrara

Alpe Apuane

Appennino Toscano

Lucca

Pistoia

Prato

Pisa

Arno

Firenze

Livorno

Volterra

Chianti

Arezzo

Maremma

Siena

Le Crete

Ombrone

Montalcino

Grosseto

Isola del Giglio

Elba

Tuscany Interiors
Intérieurs de Toscane
Toskana Interieurs

Paolo Rinaldi

Tuscany Interiors
Intérieurs de Toscane
Toskana Interieurs

Edited by | Sous la direction de | Herausgegeben von

Angelika Taschen

TASCHEN

KÖLN LISBOA LONDON NEW YORK PARIS TOKYO

Illustration page 2 | Reproduction page 2 | Abbildung Seite 2:
Detail of the home of Sandro Chia (see pp. 150–157)
Détail de la maison de Sandro Chia (voir pp. 150–157)
Detailaufnahme des Hauses von Sandro Chia (s. S. 150–157)
Photo: Simon Upton / The Interior Archive

Endpaper and page 1 | Pages de garde et page 1 | Vorsatzpapier und Seite 1:
Drawings by | Dessins par | Zeichnungen von Hervé van der Straeten, Paris

© 1998 Benedikt Taschen Verlag GmbH
Hohenzollernring 53, D-50672 Köln
Picture research by Paolo Rinaldi, Marion Hauff, Milan
Layout by Marion Hauff, Milan, Angelika Taschen, Cologne
Text edited by Ursula Fethke, Cologne
Production by Ute Wachendorf, Cologne
English translation by George Giles Watson, Udine
French translation by Pascal Varejka, Paris
German translation by Antje Longhi, Munich

Printed in Italy
ISBN 3-8228-7882-0 (English cover)
ISBN 3-8228-7722-0 (French cover)
ISBN 3-8228-7590-2 (German cover)

Contents
Sommaire
Inhalt

Tuscany – A Journey into Harmony

Photos by Gianni Berengo Gardin

La Toscane – Voyage au cœur de l'harmonie

Photos de Gianni Berengo Gardin

Toskana – Eine Reise in die Harmonie

Photos von Gianni Berengo Gardin

There is no shortage of beautiful countries in the world and each one visited leaves its own special memories. But Tuscany is a place you fall in love with at once. The region is one of Italy's greatest attractions, with its endlessly varied beauty, the stinging Tuscan wit and the infinite threads of history woven into its cultural fabric. Tuscany's country lanes are like capillaries, spreading through the land a longing for life, an emotion that flows on relentlessly even as it fades away into the far distance.

Indeed it is such a lovely region that film-makers keep coming back. The Taviani brothers, for instance, shot "The Meadow" (Il Prato), "Floréal" (Fiorile), "The Night of San Lorenzo" (La Notte di San Lorenzo) and a free adaptation of Goethe's "Wahlverwandtschaften" in Tuscany, and Bernardo Bertolucci made "Stealing Beauty" (Io ballo da sola) there. For Luchino Visconti's "Vaghe stelle dell'orsa", for James Ivory's "A Room with a View" and for "The English Patient" by Anthony Minghella, Tuscany became a gigantic film set with stunningly beautiful towns, superbly photogenic countryside and a soundtrack enriched by the biting irony of the Tuscans themselves. Andrei Tarkovsky shot many of the scenes in "Nostalghia" at Bagno Vignoni and San Galgano. Jane Campion set her film version of "Portrait of a Lady", adapted from the novel by Henry James (1843–1916), in Tuscany, and Kenneth Branagh came here to shoot some of the scenes in "Much Ado about Nothing". The Italian film "The Cyclone" (Il Ciclone) was filmed by Leonardo Pieraccioni in the Casentino district.

But many television commercials, with messages that have nothing to do with the region, have also been set in Tuscany. Many Tuscans feel offended and exploited by this, so much so that a regional law has been passed denying access to the local landscape for such purposes by declaring it copyright. Only typical local products and, of course, films will now be allowed to use the region's image.

Tuscany is a region of great charm and serenity, almost a miracle come true. And that is how it has been since the 16th century when travellers began to throng the Tuscan countryside, fascinated by its unimaginable beauty.

Beaucoup de pays sont beaux ou intéressants et chacun de ceux que nous visitons nous laisse un souvenir particulier. Mais la Toscane constitue un cas très particulier: on en tombe carrément amoureux à cause de sa beauté multiforme, de l'esprit de ses habitants, de son histoire, de sa culture et de sa cuisine. L'âme de la région est tissée d'innombrables menus événements enracinés dans un doux paysage extrêmement humanisé.

La Toscane est si belle que le cinéma ne cesse de l'exploiter. Les frères Taviani ont tourné dans la région leurs films «Le Pré» (Il Prato), «Fiorile», «La Nuit de San Lorenzo» (La Notte di San Lorenzo) et leur libre adaptation des «Affinités électives» de Goethe, et Bernardo Bertolucci y a filmé «Beauté volée» (Io ballo da sola). De «Sandra» de Luchino Visconti à «Chambre avec vue» et au «Patient anglais», la région a toujours constitué un décor très prisé pour la splendeur de ses villes et pour la douceur picturale de ses paysages. Andreï Tarkovski a tourné de nombreuses scènes de son «Nostalghia» à Bagno Vignoni et à San Galgano. Jane Campion y a situé l'adaptation cinématographique de «Portrait de femme» de l'écrivain Henry James (1843–1916), et Kenneth Branagh quelques scènes de son film «Beaucoup de bruit pour rien», tiré de la pièce de théâtre de William Shakespeare. Le film italien «Il Ciclone» a été filmé par Leonardo Pieraccioni dans la région du Casentino, près de l'ermitage de Camaldoli.

Mais on réalise également sur place de nombreux spots publicitaires dont les messages n'ont rien à voir avec la région. Les Toscans s'en sont émus au point de promulguer une loi régionale qui met le paysage toscan «sous clé» et instaure un copyright substantiel pour l'exploiter. On n'autorisera plus que la publicité des produits typiques de la région et les tournages de films.

La Toscane est tellement imprégnée de spiritualité qu'elle semble presque un miracle de l'esprit qui est devenu matière. Et elle l'a toujours été: depuis le 16e siècle, elle n'a cessé d'attirer des foules de visiteurs venus de toute l'Europe qui furent éblouis par sa beauté inimaginable et splendide.

Es gibt viele Länder und Regionen, die schön oder interessant sind und an die wir uns immer wieder gerne erinnern. Die Toskana hingegen erobert unsere Herzen im Sturm. Hier nimmt uns vieles gefangen: die facettenreiche Schönheit der Landschaft, der ganz eigene Charakter der Bewohner, die unzähligen kleinen und großen Geschichten, die sich um Kunst und Kultur ranken, und nicht zuletzt die toskanische Küche.

Die Schönheit der Toskana faszinierte auch Filmemacher immer wieder. Die Brüder Taviani haben hier zahlreiche Filme gedreht, wie »Die Wiese« (Il Prato), »Fiorile«, »Die Nacht von San Lorenzo« (La Notte di San Lorenzo) und »Wahlverwandtschaften« (Affinità elettive), eine freie Bearbeitung des Romans von Goethe. Auch »Gefühl und Verführung« (Io ballo da sola) von Bernardo Bertolucci spielt in dieser Gegend. Luchino Visconti drehte hier »Sandra« (Vaghe stelle dell'orsa), James Ivory »Zimmer mit Aussicht« und Anthony Minghella »Der englische Patient«. Seit jeher gilt die malerische Landschaft mit ihren wunderschönen Plätzen und dem weichen Licht als eine einzige großartige Kulisse. Viele Szenen von Andrej Tarkowskis »Nostalghia« entstanden in Bagno Vignoni und in San Galgano. Auch das von Jane Campion verfilmte »Bildnis einer Dame« aus der Feder des amerikanischen Schriftstellers Henry James (1843–1916) spielt in der Toskana, ebenso wie Kenneth Branaghs »Viel Lärm um Nichts« nach dem Stück von William Shakespeare. Für den letzten Film, die Komödie »Il Ciclone«, drehte Leonardo Pieraccioni 1996 im Casentino in der Nähe der Einsiedelei Camaldoli.

Allerdings entstanden auch zunehmend Werbespots, die überhaupt nichts mit der Region zu tun haben. Die Toskaner empfanden dies als Beleidigung und schrieben ein »Copyright« fest: In Zukunft dürfen hier nur noch Filme und Werbesendungen für toskanische Produkte gedreht werden.

Die Anmut der Toskana ist etwas ganz Besonderes. Hier scheint eine geistige Haltung Gestalt angenommen zu haben. Das wußten und fühlten schon seit dem 16. Jahrhundert die Reisenden aus vielen europäischen Ländern, die diese herrliche Region besuchten.

Florence – Mother of Tuscany

In order to describe Tuscany, it is necessary to begin with Florence. The people of Florence call the elegant dome that surmounts the huge bulk of their cathedral, Santa Maria in Fiore, the "cupolone". "Living in the shadow of the 'cupolone'" and "breathing the air of the 'cupolone'" are expressions that reveal an intimate, but entirely justified, local pride in a masterpiece that was built with a very Tuscan sense of proportion by Filippo Brunelleschi (1377–1446) in the first half of the 15th century.

There is no other place in the world where one can live in such close symbiosis with art as in Florence. At times it feels more like an open-air museum of the Renaissance than a city. As you wander through the alleyways between Via Tornabuoni and Via dei Calzaiuoli at night, it is easy to imagine that you have travelled back in time. Ladies and their escorts in embroidered velvet might step out of the shadows there, or appear strolling through one of the magnificent parks: Giardino dell'Iris and Giardino delle Rose in Piazzale Michelangelo, the grounds of the Villa di Castello and Villa La Petraia, or the Boboli gardens. Or you might expect to meet a courtier sauntering along the one-kilometre long corridor, now re-opened, that links Palazzo Vecchio to Palazzo Pitti. It was commissioned from the Mannerist architect Giorgio Vasari (1511–1574) by Grand Duke Cosimo I de'Medici (1519–1574) so that he could walk home from his office without going out onto the street. Vasari's corridor houses the largest collection of self-portraits in the world, including works by Raphael, Andrea del Sarto, Peter Paul Rubens and Sir Anthony van Dyck.

The history of Florence is bound up with the chronicles of the indigenous aristocracy and their vast artistic heritage. The nobles were primarily merchants and, when not involved in political activities, bought and sold corn, silk, wine, cloth and brocade in the streets and market places. The blue blood of Florence is thrifty, secretive and keeps well away from scandal and high society. One of its traditional meeting places is the Circolo dell'Unione, in Via de'Tornabuoni. Their current president is Guelfo della Gherardesca, a descendant of the notorious

Florence – mère de la Toscane

Si l'on voulait décrire la Toscane, il faudrait commencer par Florence. Les Florentins appellent «grande coupole» l'élégante coupole qui couronne l'immense masse de la cathédrale Santa Maria del Fiore. «Vivre à l'ombre du ‹cupolone›», «respirer l'air du ‹cupolone›» sont des expressions qui révèlent la fierté secrète mais sacrée des Florentins pour ce chef-d'œuvre, réalisé avec un sens de la mesure typiquement toscan par Filippo Brunelleschi (1377–1446) durant la première moitié du 15e siècle.

Il n'existe aucun autre endroit au monde où, comme à Florence, on puisse vivre aussi étroitement en symbiose avec l'art. Plus qu'une ville, il s'agit d'une sorte de musée de la Renaissance en plein air. En se promenant la nuit dans les ruelles situées entre via de'Tornabuoni et via dei Calzaiuoli, il est facile d'effectuer mentalement un voyage à rebours dans le temps et de s'attendre à voir surgir de l'obscurité des dames et des gentilshommes en habits de velours finement brodés. Il en est de même dans les magnifiques jardins de l'iris et des roses au Piazzale Michelangelo, dans ceux de Villa di Castello et de Villa La Petraia, dans ceux de Boboli; ou encore dans le corridor de Vasari, long de près d'un kilomètre, qui relie le Palazzo Vecchio au Palazzo Pitti. Construit par l'architecte Giorgio Vasari (1511–1574) pour le grand-duc Cosme Ier de Médicis (1519–1574) afin qu'il puisse se rendre de son bureau à son logis sans descendre dans la rue, ce corridor abrite la plus grande collection d'auto-portraits du monde, dont ceux de Raphaël, d'Andrea del Sarto, de Rubens et de Van Dyck.

L'histoire de Florence est toujours liée à celle de sa noblesse, riche d'un extraordinaire patrimoine historique et artistique. On ne peut dédaigner les nobles descendant de ces marchands qui, une fois réglées les affaires publiques, négociaient dans les ruelles et sur les places le blé, la soie, le vin, les étoffes et les brocarts. Le sang bleu de la «ville au lys» est parcimonieux, peu enclin au bavardage, à l'écart des scandales et des mondanités. L'un de ses lieux de prédilection est le Circolo dell'Unione, via de'Tornabuoni. L'actuel président en est Guelfo della Gherardesca, descendant du fameux comte Ugolino,

Florenz – Die Mutter der Toskana

Will man die Toskana beschreiben, so beginnt man natürlich mit Florenz. Beherrscht wird die Stadt von der imposanten Silhouette des Doms, Santa Maria del Fiore, mit der eleganten Kuppel, die die Florentiner »cupolone«, große Kuppel, nennen. »Im Schatten des ›cupolone‹ leben«, »die Nähe des ›cupolone‹ spüren« – in diesen Redewendungen kommt ein unerschütterlicher Lokalpatriotismus zum Ausdruck. Die Florentiner sind stolz auf das Meisterwerk, das Filippo Brunelleschi (1377–1446) mit »typisch toskanischem Augenmaß« in der ersten Hälfte des 15. Jahrhunderts errichtet hat.

An keinem anderen Ort der Welt lebt man so intensiv mit der Kunst wie in Florenz. Eigentlich ist die Stadt ein Freilichtmuseum mit Werken der Renaissance. In den Gäßchen zwischen der Via de'Tornabuoni und der Via dei Calzaiuoli fühlt man sich nachts in vergangene Zeiten versetzt. Jeden Augenblick könnten aus dem Halbschatten Fürsten und Prinzessinnen in fein bestickten Samtgewändern hervortreten. Auch in den herrlichen Schwertlilien- und Rosengärten am Piazzale Michelangelo, in den Gärten der Villen di Castello und La Petraia sowie in den Giardini di Boboli kann man ihre Gegenwart spüren. Oder auch in dem knapp einen Kilometer langen Verbindungsgang vom Palazzo Vecchio zum Palazzo Pitti. Den »Corridoio Vasariano« gab Großherzog Cosimo I. (1519–1574) aus dem Geschlecht der Medici bei dem berühmten Baumeister Giorgio Vasari (1511–1574) in Auftrag. Der Gang ermöglichte es den Medici, von ihrem Arbeitsplatz nach Hause zu gelangen, ohne die Straße zu betreten. Hier ist die umfangreichste Selbstporträt-Sammlung der Welt untergebracht, unter anderem mit Werken von Raffael, Andrea del Sarto, Peter Paul Rubens und Sir Anthonis van Dyck.

Die Geschichte von Florenz war und ist entscheidend mit der Aristokratie verbunden. Ursprünglich waren viele Adelige Kaufleute gewesen. Auch nachdem sie politischen Einfluß gewonnen hatten, handelten sie weiterhin in den Gäßchen und auf den Plätzen mit Getreide, Seide, Wein und Brokatstoffen. Heute sind die blaublütigen Einwohner der Stadt mit dem Lilienwappen sparsam und nicht

Conte Ugolino immortalized in Dante's "Inferno". When in prison, Ugolino was compelled by hunger to devour a "proud repast", that is to say he ate his own children (but it seems that this was a slander spread by the Pisans).

Florence's river is the Arno and no watercourse is more famed or feared. Dante himself called the Arno that "accursed and unlucky ditch" and no one has forgotten the disastrous floods of November 1966. The Arno has a long history extending from prehistoric settlements, to the Etruscans and the Romans, and from religious communities in their majestic retreats in the woods to nobles, warlords and soldiers with their castles, fortified villages and battles. The Arno's history also includes all the artists, writers and intellectuals who were born or have lived on its banks and who, over the centuries, together with craftsmen and merchants, created everything that can now be admired along the river's course from its source at Monte Falterona to the Tyrrhenian Sea.

The Chianti

The mythology surrounding Tuscany as a spiritual refuge started in Chianti. Italian and non-Italian settlers alike have a special rapport with the environment and the land. They live there despite the cold winters and isolation of its hills. Many return to the soil and take up farming. It is here that rebels, meditators, those seeking refuge from the hurly-burly of modern life and would-be latter-day hermits find a haven. They may be looking for equilibrium, independence or just for a hideaway in these verdant hills where the odd car shares the road with cyclists. It is delightful to gaze on a landscape that is familiar from Renaissance paintings. The hills look wild yet tended. Dense woodlands of oak and chestnut alternate with cypress trees and stretches of vines or olive groves. Houses built in recent centuries, small Romanesque churches and sometimes entire villages have a luminous, pale ivory or warm yellow colour. These are the shades of "alberese", the variety of chalkstone found in the area. Then there are all the towers and castles, for this was once the battlefield of Florentines and Sienese. War has left its

immortalisé dans l'«Enfer» de Dante pour avoir dévoré en prison, poussé par la faim, «un horrible repas», à savoir ses propres enfants. Il semble qu'il s'agisse en réalité d'une calomnie des Pisans.

Le fleuve qui traverse Florence est l'Arno. Il n'est pas de cours d'eau qui fasse plus jaser et qui soit plus craint que lui. Même le «divin poète» Dante l'a qualifié de «fleuve maudit et infortuné» dans son «Purgatoire» et personne n'a oublié la désastreuse inondation de 1966. Depuis l'installation des premiers hommes puis des Etrusques et des Romains, l'Arno a vu passer des religieux, des ermites installés au milieu des forêts, des seigneurs, des hobereaux et des condottieri, qui ont édifié leurs châteaux ou leurs bourgs et livré batailles sur ses rives; sans oublier les artistes et les hommes de lettres, tous les hommes de génie qui naquirent ou vécurent sur ses rives et qui ont contribué, au cours des siècles, avec les artisans et les marchands, à créer tout ce que l'on peut admirer en suivant le cours du fleuve, du mont Falterona, où il prend sa source, jusqu'à l'endroit où il se jette dans la mer Tyrrhénienne.

Le Chianti

La région du Chianti a suscité un nouvel engouement. Italiens et étrangers viennent y chercher un refuge spirituel, dans un rapport privilégié avec les lieux et la terre. Ils s'installent dans le Chianti et supportent ses hivers froids et l'isolement de ses collines. Ils ne sont pas rares à s'engager à rebours sur la voie de l'utopie, en devenant exploitants agricoles. Le Chianti attire les gens à contre-courant, les contemplatifs, ceux qui fuient le bruit, qui choisissent de vivre comme des sortes d'ermites laïcs, qui aspirent à un surplus d'équilibre et d'autonomie. Des individus qui viennent chercher un havre parmi ces vertes collines où passent de rares voitures et cyclistes. Le paysage est resté celui des tableaux de la Renaissance: des collines à la fois sauvages et domestiquées, des bois touffus de chênes et de châtaigniers, avec çà et là quelques cyprès, et des hectares de vignes et d'oliviers. Les maisons des siècles passés, les églises romanes, certains bourgs de l'intérieur sont d'un blanc ivoire cendré très

sehr gesprächig. Es gibt keine Skandale und auch
kein mondänes Gesellschaftsleben. Man trifft sich in
der Via de'Tornabuoni im Circolo dell'Unione. Der-
zeitiger Präsident des Aristokratenzirkels ist Guelfo
della Gherardesca, ein Nachfahre jenes berühmten
Grafen Ugolino, den Dante in der Hölle der »Göttlichen Komödie« verewigt hat. Es wird behauptet,
daß Ugolino im »Hungerturm« aus Verzweiflung
seine eigenen toten Söhne verschlungen habe.
Wahrscheinlich ist das jedoch eine Erfindung der
Pisaner.

Durch das Herz von Florenz fließt der Arno.
Es gibt wohl keinen Fluß, über den so viel gesagt
wurde und der so gefürchtet wird. Für Dante war er
»der unglückselige und verfluchte Graben«, und die
entsetzliche Überschwemmung vom November
1966 ist allen Bewohnern im Gedächtnis geblieben.
An seinen Ufern siedelten Menschen schon in frühe-
ster Zeit, noch vor Etruskern und Römern. Später errichteten in den Wäldern Eremiten Einsiedeleien,
während sich in den Burgen und Dörfern Adelige
und Heerführer Schlachten lieferten. Künstler, Litera-
ten und ihre Mäzene schufen gemeinsam mit Hand-
werkern und Kaufleuten entlang des Flußlaufs das
Bild, wie man es heute von der Quelle am Monte
Falterona bis zur Mündung im Tyrrhenischen Meer
bewundert.

Die Region Chianti

Der Mythos der Toskana als Ort der Kontemplation
hat seinen Ursprung im Chianti, einem Landstrich,
dem sich Italiener wie ausländische Besucher besonders verbunden fühlen. Geduldig ertragen die
hier Ansässigen die kalten, feuchten Winter und die
Einsamkeit auf den Hügeln. Nicht wenige »Aussteiger« erliegen utopischen Phantasien und versuchen
sich als Landwirte. Es sind Menschen, die Besin-
nung und Einsamkeit abseits des Großstadtlärms
suchen, die im Einklang mit der Natur und sich
selbst leben möchten. Die Landschaft wirkt noch immer wie ein Renaissancegemälde, mit wilden und
gleichzeitig sanften Hügeln, Eichen- und Kastanien-
wäldern, zwischen denen unvermittelt Zypressen
auftauchen, mit Weingärten und Olivenhainen, alten
Häusern und romanischen Pfarrkirchen. Viele Dör-

mark on the people of Chianti, who are gentle and friendly by nature, lacking the scathing irony that characterizes other Tuscans. As a group, they are hard working but not excessively so. Their love of the functional has left an almost magical imprint on the Tuscan landscape.

Florentines have always preferred properties near the city in the Impruneta area and hundreds of houses that used to belong to tenant farmers have been saved from ruin, some of them being turned into second homes. It is astonishing that property speculation should be so rife in areas of such serene, ancient beauty. The sublime beauty of Chianti is the result of age-long intervention by humanity and as such should be carefully protected.

Chianti was the first viticultural zone in the world to be defined and delimited, thanks to a decree of Grand Duke Cosimo III de'Medici (1642–1723) dating from 1716. However, cases of wine were being shipped to England as early as the previous century. The estates are almost all small and the finest wines come from grapes grown on rough, stony soils. Today the Consorzio Chianti Classico produces 22 million bottles a year.

Siena and the Crete

The Via Cassia, the road that leads from Fiesole to Rome, was paved about 180 BC by the consul, Cassius Longinus. It was partially constructed over the ancient Etruscan highway that led to the cities of Etruria and offers the traveller, especially in the province of Siena, delightful views of vines, olive trees, villas and farms, dark ranks of cypresses, ridge-top castles and villages perched on hills. The road passes in and out of age-old fortified villages through countryside as neat as a pensioner's garden. Certaldo, the birthplace of the writer Giovanni Boccaccio (1313–1375), is a muddle of steps, alleys, paved courtyards, Gothic windows and crenellations. The warm brick is set off on the far side of the walls by fields and winding lanes, vines and clusters of pines.

At last you arrive at Siena, formerly a centre of Etruscan, then Roman, civilization, built on three hills. The three main streets converge on Piazza del Campo, a square shaped like a scallop shell and

lumineux ou d'un jaune chaud. C'est dû à l'«albe-rese»(liais), une pierre calcaire locale. Partout se dressent des tours et des châteaux, car c'était le territoire que se disputaient les Florentins et les Siennois; c'est peut-être ce qui, par contraste, a rendu les natifs du Chianti doux et cordiaux, dépourvus de l'âpreté ironique des autres Toscans. Ils forment une communauté active mais non frénétique, consacrée à l'utile et au beau, qui a imposé à la nature originelle, sans la violenter, une géométrie presque irréelle. Les Florentins ont toujours acheté à proximité de leur capitale, dans la région d'Impruneta. On compte par centaines les métairies sauvées de l'abandon, en partie transformées en résidences secondaires. On n'imaginerait jamais que la spéculation immobilière puisse toucher justement ces lieux empreints d'une beauté antique et sereine. Et pourtant, cette toile peinte à l'aquarelle, si fragile, avec ses collines ourlées de cyprès, ses vignes anciennes, ses petites routes blanches sinueuses, ses tours et ses châteaux visibles de loin, est constamment égratignée. La beauté de cette région est le résultat de l'action séculaire de l'homme: on se doit de la sauvegarder.

Le Chianti a été la première zone vinicole du monde à être délimitée, grâce à un édit du grand-duc Cosme III de Médicis (1642–1723), en 1716. Mais dès le 17e siècle, on expédiait des caisses de vin en Angleterre. Il subsiste presque partout des exploitations de petites dimensions. Les sols secs et cailouteux donnent le meilleur vin. Aujourd'hui le Consorzio Chianti Classico produit 22 millions de bouteilles par an.

Sienne et le Crete
Le long de la route qui mène de Fiesole à Rome, la via Cassia, pavée vers 180 avant J.-C. par le consul Cassius Longinus – elle se superposait en partie à l'ancienne piste étrusque unissant les cités de l'Étrurie –, on voit triompher, surtout dans la province de Sienne, un paysage-mosaïque de vignobles, d'oliveraies, de villas, de fermes, de rangées sombres de cyprès, de châteaux érigés sur la ligne de faîte et de villages perchés sur de hautes collines. On pénètre dans des bourgs très anciens et on en

fer sind aus dem hell leuchtenden »alberese« erbaut, einem lokalen Kalkstein, dessen Farbe zwischen Elfenbein, Hellgrau und Warmgelb changiert. Nur selten fährt hier ein Auto, manchmal sieht man Fahrradfahrer. Vielleicht haben die blutigen Schlachten in der Vergangenheit zwischen Florentinern und Sienesen bewirkt, daß die Bewohner des Chianti heute sanft und herzlich sind. Die beißende Ironie der übrigen Toskaner geht ihnen völlig ab. Es sind fleißige, aber keine hektischen Menschen mit Sinn für das Nützliche und Schöne. Sie haben die Natur auf fast märchenhafte Weise verwandelt, ohne ihr Gewalt anzutun.

Häufig erwarben Florentiner bei Impruneta einen zweiten Wohnsitz. Auf diese Weise konnten zwar Hunderte alter Pächterhäuser vor dem Verfall gerettet werden, doch die Bauspekulation griff wie ein Feuer um sich. Das empfindliche Aquarell – die von Zypressen gesäumten Hügel, die alten Weingärten, die weißen Sträßchen, die sich durch die Landschaft schlängeln, die in der Ferne leuchtenden Türme und Burgen – wird immer wieder beschädigt. Die Schönheit des Chianti wurde im Laufe vieler Jahrhunderte geschaffen, und es gilt, sie zu bewahren.

Der Chianti war das erste Weinbaugebiet der Welt, dessen Grenzen genau festgelegt wurden. Dies erfolgte 1716 durch eine Verordnung des Großherzogs Cosimo III. (1642–1723). Aber schon im 17. Jahrhundert wurde Wein nach England exportiert. Auch kleine Winzer konnten sich in der Toskana halten, denn auf dem harten, steinigen Boden lassen sich hervorragende Weine anbauen. Heute erzeugt die Winzergenossenschaft Consorzio Chianti Classico 22 Millionen Flaschen im Jahr.

Siena und die Crete
Bereits um 180 v. Chr. ließ der römische Konsul Cassius Longinus die Via Cassia anlegen. Sie führt teilweise auf einer alten Etruskerstraße von Fiesole nach Rom. Heute beeindruckt links und rechts der Via Cassia die an ein Mosaik erinnernde Landschaft der Provinz Siena: Weingärten, Olivenhaine, Villen und Landgüter, dunkle Zypressenalleen, hochgelegene Burgen und Dörfer ziehen vorüber. Über Fel-

dominated by the Palazzo Pubblico that incorporates the Torre del Mangia. The Council Chamber of the Palazzo Pubblico is dominated by the "Maestà", or Virgin Enthroned in Glory, of Simone Martini (c. 1284–1344), one of the greatest artists of the Italian Gothic style. Siena is above all the home of the Palio horserace, a tradition that is re-enacted twice each year in Piazza del Campo. A focus for local rivalries, it is an integral part of the life of the community.

To the south are the wonderful Crete, Siena's clay hills that stand as bare as the dunes of the Sahara in subtly shaded, pastel colours. Romanesque churches and flocks of sheep nestle peacefully in the folds of the Crete. There too, the silent abbey of Monte Oliveto Maggiore, built in the 14th century, with frescoes by Il Sodoma (1477–1549) and Luca Signorelli (c. 1445–1523), stands sentinel, rugged and aloof. Fitting neighbours are the roofless abbey of San Galgano and the famous chapel of Montesiepi where the legendary sword of Saint Galgano was thrust into the rock.

Arezzo is also a citadel of art. Standing on a hill from which it dominates four different valleys, the city can be seen from a long way off. It has been coveted for its strategic position since Etruscan times. In the days of the medieval Italian states, being a Ghibelline stronghold for the emperor's faction, it was in eternal conflict with Guelph Florence, to whom it was forced to surrender after the rout of Campaldino in 1289. All the harmony of a city that has matured slowly but surely over the ages is concentrated in its Piazza Grande: crenellated towers, medieval wooden balconies, a Romanesque apse and 16th-century fountain, and the palazzo and loggias of Giorgio Vasari who, like the poet Francesco Petrarca (1304–1374), was one of Arezzo's famous sons. Piero della Francesca (c. 1415/20–1492), born at Borgo Sansepolcro, also left his mark in a cycle of frescoes in the basilica of San Francesco. These masterpieces invite the visitor to view the places they depict in the countryside around Arezzo, a gentler, more peaceful area of Tuscany: Citerna, with its tower, Monterchi, atop a sheer cliff, Anghiari, with narrow streets winding around the Palazzo del Comune, and stunning, medieval Borgo Sansepol-

ressort par des portes, au milieu d'une campagne aménagée comme un jardin. Certaldo est la patrie de l'écrivain Boccace (1313–1375), toute en pentes, en ruelles, en escaliers, en cours pavées, en petites fenêtres gothiques et en crénelures, dominée par le coloris chaud de la brique; et au-delà des pans de la muraille, ce sont encore des champs et des sentiers, des vignes et des pins maritimes.

Ancien centre étrusque puis colonie romaine, Sienna a été modelée par les plis de trois collines. Les trois voies les plus importantes convergent vers la piazza del Campo, une place en forme de valve de coquillage dominée par le Palazzo Pubblico, avec la Torre del Mangia. Dans la salle du Conseil du Palazzo Pubblico, la «Vierge en majesté» de Simone Martini (vers 1284–1344), un des plus grands peintres du gothique italien, apparaît dans toute sa splendeur. Mais Sienne, c'est surtout le Palio, la course aux chevaux, une tradition qui est suivie deux fois par an sur la place, centre des passions citadines; le Palio est un moment essentiel de la vie de la communauté.

Non loin de Sienne s'étendent les magiques Crete Senesi, des collines désolées comme des dunes sahariennes, aux tons tamisés, estompés; c'est un univers ponctué d'églises romanes et de troupeaux de brebis en train de paître devant la silencieuse abbaye de Monte Oliveto Maggiore, construite au 14e siècle dans un lieu sauvage et inaccessible, qui abrite des fresques de Sodoma (1477–1549) et de Luca Signorelli (vers 1445–1523). On découvre l'abbaye sans toit de San Galgano, où l'herbe pousse entre les fissures du pavement. Tout près de là se trouve la chapelle de Montesiepi avec l'épée légendaire de saint Galgano enfoncée dans la roche.

Arezzo est également une ville d'art. Elle se voit de loin, perchée sur une colline d'où elle domine les accès à quatre vallées. Sa position stratégique attisait déjà les convoitises à l'époque des Etrusques. Durant la querelle des Investitures et les luttes des Communes Libres, Arezzo appartenait au parti gibelin, partisan de l'Empire. Après la défaite de Campaldino en 1289, la ville dut s'incliner devant Florence, qui au contraire était guelfe et

der, die wie Gärten anmuten, gelangt man zu den antiken Stadttoren kleiner Ortschaften: beispielsweise nach Certaldo, wo der Dichter und Humanist Giovanni Boccaccio (1313–1375) geboren wurde. Zahlreiche Treppchen, kleine Gassen, gepflasterte Höfe, gotische Fenster und Zinnenkränze prägen den Ort. Die Ziegelsteine leuchten in warmen Farben, und jenseits der Mauern blickt man auf Strandkiefern, Weinberge und von Wegen durchzogene Felder.

Schließlich erreicht man das auf drei Hügeln errichtete Siena, einst etruskische, dann römische Stadt. Drei Hauptstraßen führen auf die Piazza del Campo, deren Form an eine Muschel erinnert und die vom Palazzo Pubblico mit der Torre del Mangia beherrscht wird. Im Ratssaal des Palazzo Pubblico bewundert man die »Maestà«, die thronende Madonna mit Kind, von Simone Martini (um 1284–1344), einem Hauptvertreter der gotischen Malerei Italiens. Aber Siena – das ist vor allem der Palio, ein zweimal jährlich auf der Piazza del Campo stattfindendes Pferderennen. Er stellt das städtische Ereignis überhaupt dar, an dem sich die Leidenschaften sämtlicher Einwohner entzünden.

Südlich von Siena liegen die »Crete«, eine beeindruckende Landschaft mit spärlich bewachsenen Hügeln aus aschgrauem bis gelbem Ton – eine Landschaft, die an die Dünen der Sahara erinnert. Hier weiden Schafe neben romanischen Kirchen. Auf einem Felsvorsprung thront einsam die Abtei Monte Oliveto Maggiore aus dem 14. Jahrhundert mit den Fresken von Sodoma (1477–1549) und Luca Signorelli (um 1445–1523). Berühmt sind auch die Ruinen der Zisterzienserabtei San Galgano, deren Dach fehlt und wo Grasbüschel zwischen den Spalten des Fußbodens wachsen. Ganz in der Nähe liegt die Kapelle von Montesiepi, in der das in einem Felsblock steckende, mythische Schwert des Heiligen Galgano aufbewahrt wird.

Auch Arezzo ist reich an Kunstschätzen. Die hochgelegene Stadt kontrolliert den Zugang zu vier Tälern und war deshalb schon zur Zeit der Etrusker von strategischer Bedeutung. Während des Investiturstreits und der Kämpfe zwischen den italienischen Stadtrepubliken unterstützte Arezzo die kaisertreuen Ghibellinen, bis es 1289 von dem papstfreundlichen,

cro with its noble palazzo that was once the home of Piero della Francesca. The museum there contains, not only his superb polyptych, but the "Resurrection", described by the English writer Aldous Huxley as "the most beautiful painting in the world". Peaceful and pleasant olive groves and lines of cypresses lead you to the chapel of Monterchi, hidden in the fields. Inside, two angels draw aside the edges of a damask curtain to reveal the celebrated "Madonna del Parto", or pregnant Virgin, a noble countrywoman dressed in blue, with an intensely mystical mien.

Montalcino and the Maremma

We have almost reached the boundary between the worlds of noise and silence, in and out of time. We are approaching Montalcino, and the legendary Monte Amiata. Known to locals simply as "la Montagna", the Mountain, this imposing, extinct volcano from the Quaternary period rises up between the valleys of the Orcia, Fiora and Paglia. Its ancient fascination is interwoven with a history that revolves around the mysterious metal – mercury – concealed in its depths. The landscape is often shrouded in mists, under a near-white sky tinged with ochre, brown, rust and yellow, and hills mottled with olives. On jutting outcrops of tufa, long-forgotten medieval villages stand in silent stillness gazing over breathtaking panoramas of thin snaking rivers and weatherbeaten purple earth. Pitigliano, built on a cliff then slowly piled on top of itself, was begun in the days of the Etruscans, who carved grottoes and tombs out of the rock. It reached the heights of Renaissance splendour under the Orsini, a princely Roman family. Winds from a bygone Maremma also blow through the travertine portals, past the wells, washing troughs, roof-terraces and medieval fortified houses of Sorano. Sovana, another ancient town, clinging to its rock, has a tiny brick-paved square, two churches and a few noble residences, and all around, roads lead off to Etruscan necropolises. Between Montalcino and Montepulciano lies Pienza, the city built by 15th-century princes and architects in accordance with their philosophical ideals, which has remained intact ever since. It was Enea Silvio Piccolomini (1405–1464) who, when he

soutenait la papauté. Toute l'harmonie d'une ville qui s'est développée avec sagesse est condensée sur la piazza Grande, avec ses tours crénelées et ses balcons médiévaux de bois, son abside romane et sa fontaine du 16e siècle, son palais et ses arcades de Giorgio Vasari, illustre fils de la ville, comme le poète Pétrarque (1304–1374). Quant à Piero della Francesca (vers 1415/20–1492), né à Borgo Sansepolcro, il laissa à la ville un cycle de fresques dans la basilique San Francesco. Ses merveilleuses fresques incitent d'ailleurs à visiter les lieux proches d'Arezzo qu'il a dépeints, où la campagne est plus douce et austère: les villages de Citerna avec son donjon, de Monterchi perché au sommet d'une colline escarpée, d'Anghiari avec ses étroites ruelles en colimaçon qui rayonnent autour du Palazzo del Comune, et de Borgo Sansepolcro, merveilleusement médiéval, avec le palais nobiliaire qui fut la demeure de Piero della Francesca. Là, le musée municipal abrite, outre son superbe «Polyptique de la Miséricorde», sa «Résurrection», que l'écrivain anglais Aldous Huxley a qualifiée de «plus beau tableau du monde». Dans un cadre simple et serein, des étendues d'oliviers et des rangées de cyprès mènent à la chapelle de Monterchi, au milieu des champs où, dans une simplicité dépouillée, entre deux anges qui écartent les pans d'un rideau en damas, apparaît la célèbre «Madonna del Parto», une noble paysanne entièrement vêtue de bleu clair, image mystique d'une intensité extraordinaire.

Montalcino et la Maremme

Nous avons désormais atteint la limite entre l'univers intense du bruit et du temps qui s'écoule et le monde simple, silencieux et atemporel des campagnes isolées. Nous sommes proches de Montalcino, autour du mythique Monte Amiata, que les gens du pays appellent simplement «la Montagna», un imposant volcan éteint du quaternaire. Il se dresse, tout seul, entre les vallées de l'Orcia, du Fiora et du Paglia, auréolé d'une antique fascination et d'une longue histoire qui s'est souvent identifiée au cours des millénaires avec celle du mystérieux métal enfoui dans ses entrailles, le mercure. Sous un ciel presque blanc, le paysage, souvent voilé de

guelfischen Florenz in der Schlacht bei Campaldino besiegt wurde. Die Harmonie der sukzessive gewachsenen Stadt wird auf der Piazza Grande besonders deutlich. Hier fügen sich zinnenbekrönte Türme, mittelalterliche Holzbalkone, eine romanische Apsis, ein Brunnen aus dem 16. Jahrhundert und der Palazzo delle Loggie zu einem ausgewogenen Ganzen. Letzterer wurde entworfen von Giorgio Vasari, der aus Arezzo stammt, wie auch der Dichter Francesco Petrarca (1304–1374). Wichtig für die Stadt war auch Piero della Francesca (um 1410/20–1492), der den wundervollen Freskenzyklus zur »Kreuzeslegende« in der Basilika San Francesco malte.

Seine einfühlsamen Stadtansichten verleiten den Betrachter zu einer Entdeckungsreise in die sanften, stillen Dörfer an der Grenze zu Umbrien: Citerna mit seinem hohen Turm, das auf einem steilen Hügel gelegene Monterchi, Anghiari mit den engen Serpentinen um den Palazzo Comunale und das mittelalterliche Juwel Borgo Sansepolcro mit dem Adelspalast, in dem Piero della Francesca lebte. In der dortigen Pinacoteca Comunale sind sein frühes Polyptychon »Schutzmantelmadonna und Heilige« und die »Auferstehung Christi« zu bewundern, die der englische Schriftsteller Aldous Huxley einmal als »das schönste Gemälde der Welt« bezeichnet hat.

Durch eine friedvolle, heitere Landschaft, vorbei an Olivenhainen und Zypressen, führt der Weg von Arezzo zum nahegelegenen Friedhof von Monterchi. In der schmucklosen Friedhofskapelle malte Piero della Francesca seine berühmte »Madonna del Parto«: zwei Engel schieben die Vorhänge eines Zeltraumes beiseite, in dem die schwangere Maria steht, eine mystische Figur von außerordentlicher Intensität.

Montalcino und die Maremma

Bei Montalcino verläuft die Grenze zwischen der »lauten« und der »stillen« Toskana. Wir lassen das pulsierende Leben hinter uns und treten über die Schwelle der einfachen Dinge und einsam gelegenen Landschaften. Das Land wird beherrscht vom mythischen Monte Amiata, der von den Einheimischen einfach »La Montagna«, der Berg, genannt wird. Dieser mächtige erloschene Vulkan aus dem Quar-

became Pope Pius II in 1458, wished to infuse his humble birthplace with more dignity. He set about transforming a medieval village into a utopian city, commissioning the humanist, artist and theorist Leon Battista Alberti (1404–1472) and the architect and sculptor Bernardo Rossellino (1409–1464) to build it, and so the village of Corsignano became Pienza.

The boundaries of the Maremma are mentioned by Dante at the beginning of the thirteenth canto of the "Inferno": Cecina to the north and Corneto to the south, an inhospitable territory roamed by wild beasts. Now at last designated a regional nature reserve, the nine thousand hectares, lying between the Uccellina hills and the shore, form one of the last and most spectacular stretches of virgin coastline in Italy. The park offers, in a microcosm, all that is required to create an authentically Italian Wild West: land, water, distant horizons, melancholy solitude, herds of long-horned cattle and horseback "butteri", descendants of the cowboys who outrode the legendary Buffalo Bill in 1911.

Travelling along the coast we reach the island of Elba, also a part of Tuscany. Its crystal clear waters, hidden bays enclosing inviting beaches, and mountain peaks, woods and vineyards make it a treasure trove of surprises and delights. Not to mention the excellent local cuisine and good island wine. The other islands in the Tuscan archipelago are equally enticing. Giannutri, to the south, for example, forms a half moon, lying off the Monte Argentario like a stone sabre flung out into the water.

Tuscany is a land of diversity and the "Livornesi" – the inhabitants of Leghorn – demand to be considered a race apart. Their ancestors arrived from the sea and they themselves are generous, courageous and never afraid to speak their mind. The city has no armorial bearings but it does have a proud seafaring tradition. Its streets are criss-crossed by "fossi", canals excavated by the Medicis that inevitably remind visitors of Venice. Leghorn is a town that should be explored by walking around the markets and watching the master carpenters getting the neighbourhood vessel ready for the "palio

vapeurs, revêt des tons brûlés, ocre et marron, rouille et jaune, entre les collines et les damiers des oliveraies; d'antiques bourgs oubliés s'accrochent à des éperons de tuf, dans le silence immobile, d'où l'on découvre des panoramas splendides et désolés, ouverts sur des cours d'eau étiques et des vallées à la terre corrodée et violacée. Le village de Pitigliano, édifié au bord d'un précipice, s'est lentement développé au même endroit depuis les Etrusques, qui creusèrent des grottes et des tombes dans le massif de tuf. C'est à la Renaissance, sous les Orsini, famille princière romaine, que le village atteignit l'apogée de sa splendeur. Les portails de travertin, les puits, les lavoirs, les belvédères des bourgs de Sorano, avec ses maisons-tours médiévales, et de Sovrana, blotti sur un rocher autour d'une minuscule place de brique, de deux églises et de quelques palais nobiliaires, témoignent d'un riche passé. Et partout d'antiques voies sacrées mènent aux tombes étrusques. Enfin, entre Montalcino et Montepulciano, se trouve Pienza, la cité idéale des princes et des architectes du 15e siècle, restée intacte jusqu'à nos jours. C'est Enea Silvio Piccolomini (1405–1464), devenu pape Pie II en 1458, qui voulut conférer à son lieu de naissance une nouvelle dignité, transformant le village médiéval, face au Monte Amiata, en une cité idéale; il en confia la tâche à Leon Battista Alberti (1404–1472) et à l'architecte et sculpteur Bernardo Rossellino (1409–1464). C'est ainsi que Corsignano devint Pienza.

Dante indique les limites de la Maremme au début du treizième chant de l'«Enfer»: Cecina au nord et Corneto au sud, un territoire inhospitalier où les animaux sauvages règnent en maîtres, et divisé en Maremme de Grosseto, de Livourne et de Pise. Transformés finalement en parc naturel régional, les neuf mille hectares qui s'étendent entre les collines de l'Uccellina et la mer sont l'un des derniers et des plus spectaculaires exemples de paysage côtier intact en Italie. Le parc abrite, dans un microcosme parfait, les éléments constitutifs d'un authentique Far West italien, composé de terre et d'eau, d'horizons lointains, de solitudes mélancoliques, de troupeaux de vaches aux longues cornes, de «butteri», des gardiens de bestiaux à cheval, héritiers de ceux

tär, der sich zwischen den Tälern der Flüsse Orcia, Fiora und Paglia erhebt, hat seit jeher die Menschen fasziniert. Um ihn ranken sich jahrtausendealte Geschichten, wobei das hier gewonnene Quecksilber eine wichtige Rolle spielt. Unter einem fast weißen Himmel verhüllen häufig Dämpfe die Landschaft mit ihren Goldbrauntönen: Ocker, Dunkelbraun, Rostrot und Gelb. Unvermittelt tauchen steile Felsvorsprünge aus Tuffstein auf, auf denen alte, fast vergessene Dörfer thronen. Von dort blickt man weit über die Hügel hinweg und wird doch ein wenig melancholisch, angesichts der violett schimmernden, trockenen Talböden und der Flüsse, die kaum Wasser führen.

Eines der hochgelegenen Dörfer ist das im Laufe der Jahrhunderte langsam gewachsene Pitigliano. Schon die Etrusker schlugen hier Höhlen und Grabkammern in den Tuffstein. Seine Glanzzeit erlebte der Ort in der Renaissance, als er zum Besitz des römischen Adelsgeschlechts der Orsini gehörte. Auch in Sorano mit seinen Travertinportalen, Brunnen, Waschplätzen, Balkonen und mittelalterlichen Turmbauten scheint die Vergangenheit aufzuerstehen. Sovana ist ebenfalls ein alter Ort, in dem sich seit jeher Häuser, zwei Kirchen und einige Adelspaläste dicht um einen ziegelgepflasterten Platz drängen. Und überall führen Wege zu den Nekropolen der Etrusker. Zwischen Montalcino und Montepulciano liegt Pienza, das seit dem 15. Jahrhundert unverändert geblieben ist. Ursprünglich hieß der Ort im Orcia-Tal Corsignano, doch als Pius II. (1405–1464) den Papstthron bestieg, benannte er seinen Geburtsort um und gestaltete ihn völlig neu. So entstand unter Mithilfe des Humanisten und Kunsttheoretikers Leon Battista Alberti (1404–1472) sowie des Baumeisters Bernardo Rossellino (1409–1464) die Idealstadt Pienza.

Zu Beginn des Dreizehnten Gesangs der Hölle in der »Göttlichen Komödie« setzte Dante die Grenzen der Maremma fest: im Norden Cecina, im Süden Corneto, dazwischen ein ungastliches Gebiet mit wilden Tieren. Heute teilt sich die toskanische Maremma in die Maremma Grossetana, Maremma Livornese und Maremma Pisana auf. Der Regionalpark zwischen der Uccellina-Hügelkette und dem

marinaro", a boat race that takes place during the summer. Built to plans drawn up by an architect the Medicis had selected, Leghorn was to be a model port. Its liberal statutes attracted people of all races and faiths to a city embodying rigorous town planning, tolerance and a wealth of contradictory trends.

Pisa

Pisa is famous for its two universities and the students who give the city its lively atmosphere and reputation for rebellion and protest. You bump into undergraduates everywhere, in the backstreets near the medieval market in the old quarter, or under the porticos of Borgo Stretto, in the vicinity of churches that have made Pisan architecture familiar all over the world. In the opinion of the writer Antonio Tabucchi, himself from Pisa, Piazza dei Miracoli is "ravishing, but captures the tourist's attention and leaves no space for anything else". There are of course other treasures. Outside Pisa you can visit the Roman basilica of San Piero a Grado, the estate of San Rossore, the park of Migliarino, and Torre del Lago Puccini. Here the composer Giacomo Puccini (1858–1924) built a villa with his earnings from the opera "Manon Lescaut", a villa that now houses his museum.

Montecatini, too, set in a low-lying part of the Val di Nievole at the very edge of the Apennines, has remained almost unchanged for a hundred years. Water is the predominant element shaping the style and cosmopolitan atmosphere of the spa town. Finally San Miniato, near Empoli, has three squares on top of one another, with churches, flights of steps, archways and views of exceptional beauty. From the highest of the squares, Prato del Duomo, you can see the river Arno sparkling as it winds through infinite shades of green, catch glimpses of Fiesole and Volterra, and admire the Apennines soaring up to touch the sky.

La Lucchesia

Each part of Tuscany is associated with a specific type of personality. People from Lucca, for example, are passionate yet circumspect in their behaviour. During the Renaissance sumptuary laws were enfor-

qui en 1911 surpassèrent en adresse le légendaire Buffalo Bill.

En longeant la côte, nous devons nous rappeler que la Toscane, c'est aussi l'île d'Elbe, avec sa mer limpide et transparente, ses criques secrètes et ses plages accueillantes, ses sommets abrupts, ses bois, ses vignobles généreux, sa terre pleine de surprises et de merveilles, sans oublier sa cuisine savoureuse et son excellent vin. L'archipel toscan compte d'autres îles, parmi lesquelles Giannutri, la plus méridionale, une demi-lune longue de quelques kilomètres, sorte de fragment d'écueil jeté au large de Monte Argentario.

La Toscane est le pays de la diversité. Les Livournais eux-mêmes prétendent être différents, avec des ancêtres venus de la mer, généreux, directs et courageux. Dépourvue de titre de noblesse, leur ville est cependant fière de ses traditions maritimes: elle est entrecoupée par les «fossi», les canaux des Médicis, qui évoquent un peu Venise. Il faut découvrir Livourne en flânant sur les marchés, en observant les maîtres charpentiers experts qui préparent le bateau du quartier pour le «palio marinaro» de l'été. Conçue par un architecte des Médicis, qui voulaient disposer d'un port modèle, Livourne a été édifiée par des gens de toutes races et de toutes religions, attirés par des lois très libérales; c'est un exemple unique d'urbanisme rigoureux, de tolérance et de contradictions.

Pise

Pise est célèbre pour ses deux universités. Les étudiants constituent en effet l'âme de la ville, toujours rebelle et contestataire. On les rencontre partout, dans les ruelles proches du vieux marché, la partie la plus médiévale de la ville, sous les arcades de Borgo Stretto, autour des églises qui ont rendu le style pisan célèbre dans le monde entier. Pour l'écrivain Antonio Tabucchi, lui-même né à Pise, la piazza dei Miracoli, est «magnifique, mais elle attire de manière irrésistible l'attention du touriste et ne laisse de place à rien d'autre». Mais Pise possède d'autres trésors, hors de la ville, comme la basilique romane de San Piero a Grado, le domaine de San Rossore, le parc de Migliarino et Torre del Lago

Meer, der neuntausend Hektar umfaßt, zählt zu den letzten und beeindruckendsten unberührten Küstenabschnitten Italiens. Land und Wasser, weite Horizonte, melancholische Einsamkeit, »butteri«, berittene Viehhüter, und Herden von Langhornrindern lassen den Park wie eine italienische Miniaturausgabe des Wilden Westens wirken. So ist es nicht verwunderlich, daß die toskanischen »Cowboys« den legendären Buffalo Bill an Geschicklichkeit übertrafen, der 1911 mit seiner Wildwestschau nach Europa kam.

Auch Elba mit dem türkisblauen Meer, den versteckten Buchten, den einladenden Stränden, den steilen Felsen, den Wäldern und den üppigen Weingärten gehört zum toskanischen Archipel. Hier kann man hervorragend essen und guten Wein trinken. Die südlichste toskanische Insel, Giannutri, ist mehrere Kilometer lang und wirkt wie ein halbmondförmiger Felsbrocken, der von Monte Argentario ins Meer geschleudert wurde.

Die Toskana ist die Region der Gegensätze. Die Einwohner von Livorno behaupten spöttisch von sich, großzügig, direkt und mutig zu sein, weil ihre Vorfahren über das Meer eingewandert sind. Hier gibt es keine Wappen adeliger Familien, sondern die Geschichte der Stadt wird von seiner Rolle als Hafenstadt bestimmt. Zwischen den verschiedenen Stadtteilen verlaufen die von den Medici angelegten »fossi«, kleine Kanäle, die an Venedig denken lassen. Am besten lernt man die Stadt kennen, wenn man sich auf den Märkten umsieht oder die Zimmerleute beobachtet, die das Boot ihres Viertels für den im Sommer stattfindenden »palio marinaro«, die Regatta, vorbereiten. Livorno wurde als Modellhafen von einem Baumeister der Medici entworfen. Damals zog die liberale Gesetzgebung Menschen unterschiedlicher Herkunft und diverser Glaubensrichtungen an, und auch heute noch zeichnet sich Livorno durch eine ungewöhnliche Mischung aus urbanistischer Strenge, menschlicher Toleranz und zahlreichen Widersprüchen aus.

Pisa

Pisa ist bekannt für seine beiden Universitäten. Die Studenten sind die Seele dieser Stadt, rebellisch und

ced in the city which forbade an ostentatious show of wealth or luxurious habits. These edicts applied to the exteriors of the houses but certainly not to what went on inside. Viewed from the outside, Lucca is a sober, austere city with a minimalist tendency towards moderation and reserve. It is also a very rich town, however, and has been since the days when it was the only republic whose coinage circulated throughout Europe. There are artistic wonders hidden away in the palazzi of the city and in villas on the hillsides which are rarely displayed. The people of Lucca have always jealously guarded their privacy. They were Guelphs and supporters of the pope but at the same time had friendly relations with the emperor so that they could enjoy his protection against the reviled Pisans. For the same reason, they were also allies of Genoa. And it was to keep all these enemies, including the feared Florentines, at bay that from the 15th to the 17th centuries the inhabitants of Lucca busied themselves building a superb ring of city walls with an embankment from which it was possible to see at a single glance all Lucca. The view also embraces the holm oak-crowned tower of the rich Guinigi family of merchants, the great statue of the Archangel Michael rising above the façade of San Michele in Foro, and the delicate tracery of the bell tower of San Frediano. The city invites the visitor to meditate on the continuity of past and present. More than other cities in Italy, it manages to live in harmony with its history and traditions. "It never suffered devastation, invasion or other traumas", explains the writer Francesca Duranti. "Its massive walls, perfectly conserved and perfectly useless, never sustained an assault because the people of Lucca, whom trade, manufacture and farming had made wealthy, preferred to pay."

There are other treasures to be found near Lucca, such as the church of Gattaiola, a marvellous example of Romanesque architecture. On the road to Altopascio lies Montecarlo, originally settled by the Lombards, and a jewel of a building from the 18th century, the tiny Teatro dei Rassicurati. Many small churches grace the region of Brancoleria, while Bagni di Lucca has thermal waters whose illustrious customers included the French writer Michel

Puccini, où le compositeur Giacomo Puccini (1858–1924) acheta, avec l'argent que lui avait rapporté «Manon Lescaut», la villa aujourd'hui transformée en musée commémoratif.

Quant à Montecatini, qui s'étend sur un secteur assez plat du Val di Nievole, à l'extrême limite de l'Apennin, elle est pratiquement restée inchangée par rapport à ce qu'elle était au tournant du 19e et du 20e siècle: un des hauts lieux du thermalisme, dont elle conserve le style, l'aspect, l'ambiance cosmopolite, l'atmosphère. Enfin, San Miniato, à côté d'Empoli, compte trois places superposées, agrémentées d'églises, d'escaliers monumentaux et de grandes voûtes. Elles offrent des points de vue somptueux: de la place supérieure, le Prato del Duomo, on voit l'Arno scintiller de mille nuances de vert et on entrevoit Fiesole, Volterra et l'Apennin où la terre tend à s'unir au ciel.

La province de Lucques
Chacun, en Toscane, possède son propre caractère: les Lucquois sont fougueux mais prudents. A Lucques, durant la Renaissance, on avait promulgué des lois somptuaires qui interdisaient l'étalage du luxe et de la richesse. Sur les façades, mais certainement pas à l'intérieur des maisons. Extérieurement, Lucques est une ville sobre et minimaliste, modérée et réservée. Mais elle est également très riche et elle l'a toujours été: c'est la seule République maritime qui ait réussi à imposer sa propre monnaie dans toute l'Europe. Les palais de la ville et les villas des collines environnantes recèlent des trésors artistiques rarement présentés au public. Les Lucquois ont toujours été extrêmement jaloux de leur intimité. Ils étaient guelfes et partisans du pape, mais également amis de l'empereur pour jouir de sa protection contre les Pisans abhorrés, et pour la même raison alliés à Gênes. Pour se défendre de tout le monde, y compris des Florentins qu'ils redoutaient, ils érigèrent entre le 15e et le 17e siècle ce chef-d'œuvre d'enceinte, avec un terre-plein pavé d'où l'on a la possibilité de jeter un coup d'œil circulaire sur la ville, la tour Guinigi couronnée de chênes, la grande statue de l'archange saint Michel qui surmonte la façade de San Michele in Foro, et le clocher ajouré

stets zum Widerstand bereit. Man trifft sie in den kleinen Gäßchen rings um den alten Markt im mittelalterlichen Teil der Stadt, unter den Arkaden des Borgo Stretto oder in der Nähe der Kirchen, die den Pisaner Stil in der ganzen Welt berühmt gemacht haben. Für den aus Pisa stammenden Schriftsteller Antonio Tabucchi ist die Piazza dei Miracoli, der Domplatz, zwar »wunderschön, aber die Touristen sind von ihr so fasziniert, daß sie nichts weiteres mehr sehen«. Aber natürlich gibt es noch weiteres zu entdecken: die romanische Basilika San Piero a Grado außerhalb der Stadt an der einstigen Arnomündung, den Landsitz in San Rossore, der ehemals dem Königshaus Savoyen gehörte, den Park von Migliarino und schließlich die Villa Torre del Lago Puccini. Hier wohnte und arbeitete der Komponist Giacomo Puccini (1858–1924), der die Villa mit dem Geld erwarb, das er für »Manon Lescaut« erhalten hatte. Heute befindet sich hier ein Museum.

Auch in Montecatini, das im Val di Nievole am Fuß des Apennin liegt, hat sich seit der Jahrhundertwende wenig verändert. Die Stadt hat es verstanden, Architektur, kosmopolitisches Ambiente und Atmosphäre eines eleganten Kurorts zu erhalten. In San Miniato bei Empoli schließlich entdeckt der Besucher drei übereinanderliegende Plätze, Kirchen, zahlreiche Treppen, imposante Gewölbe und Ausblicke von hinreißender Schönheit. Von dem am höchsten gelegenen Platz aus, dem Prato del Duomo, sieht man den Arno im Grün der Landschaft glitzern, man blickt auf Fiesole, Volterra und den Apennin, wo Himmel und Erde sich vereinen.

Die Lucchesia

Den Bürgern jeder einzelnen toskanischen Stadt werden ganz bestimmte Charaktereigenschaften zugeschrieben. Von den Einwohnern Luccas sagt man, sie seien feurig, aber gleichzeitig zurückhaltend. In der Renaissance war das öffentliche Zurschaustellen von Luxus und Reichtum verboten. Dies betraf allerdings nicht die Innenausstattung der Häuser. Äußerlich wirkt Lucca deshalb auch heute noch auf den Besucher nüchtern, bescheiden und maßvoll. Die Stadt ist jedoch sehr wohlhabend und ist es immer gewesen. Als einzige Stadtrepublik prägte sie Mün-

de Montaigne (1533–1592) and the German poet Heinrich Heine (1797–1856). Then there are the villas, an architectural heritage and living witness of another way of life. As many as 550, 120 of which are on a monumental scale, are to be found in a small geographical area. Some date from the 14th century, others from only a hundred years ago, but the golden age of villa building was the 16th century.

The province of Lucca offers many less well-known landscapes to the unhurried visitor. One of these is the Garfagnana area, its great walls of white marble scarred by quarries that, when seen in the distance, look as if they are covered in snow. These are the Apuan mountains, which in fact are nothing like the Apennines. Their naked peaks, steep scree slopes, ridges and sheer walls more closely resemble the Alps. The many roads and trails leading into the coastal range were built for transporting the marble blocks. The quarries themselves are awesome, some towering overhead in a white cascade of marble and others barely visible through a crack in the rock.

So Tuscany is a peaceful place, but one that still guards its precious secret. What is the source of the fascination the region has held – and continues to hold – for so many writers and artists, for distinguished figures from the past and ordinary people today, and for visitors from near and far? Is it perhaps Tuscany's natural beauty and climate, or the signs of the past and the efforts that have been made to build a better future, or is it an awareness of the region's enormous heritage in stone and sentiment? The sumptuous images in this volume can be "read" like detailed descriptions of life as it is lived today, and as it was in days gone by. Human activity has found a way to co-exist harmoniously with the land that brought it forth, or where it chose to settle. Existential despair seems to slip away here, as it does for the young hero of the epistolary novel "The Last Letters of Jacopo Ortis" (1802) by the Italian writer Ugo Foscolo. The miracle has happened before, it happens today, and it will happen again to anyone else who decides to embark on a "journey into harmony" and come to Tuscany.

comme de la dentelle de San Frediano. Lucques incite à méditer sur la continuité entre le passé et le présent: plus que d'autres villes italiennes, elle cohabite harmonieusement avec son histoire et ses traditions. «C'est parce qu'elle n'a jamais eu à subir ni destruction, ni invasions, ni traumatismes – explique la romancière Francesca Duranti. Ses murailles massives, parfaitement conservées et parfaitement inutiles, n'ont jamais subi une seule attaque, parce que les Lucquois, grâce à la richesse qu'ils tiraient du commerce, de l'artisanat et de l'agriculture, préféraient payer».

Les environs de Lucques recèlent également de nombreux trésors, comme l'église de Gattaiola, un joyau de l'architecture romane. En direction d'Altopascio, on rencontre Montecarlo, d'origine lombarde, avec son minuscule théâtre des Rassicurati, une adorable bonbonnière du 18e siècle. Beaucoup d'églises anciennes subsistent dans la zone de la Brancoliera où se trouvent les célèbres sources thermales de Bagni di Lucca, que fréquentèrent l'écrivain Michel de Montaigne (1533–1592) et l'écrivain allemand Heinrich Heine (1797–1856). Enfin la région possède un patrimoine architectural riche et surprenant qui constitue également un important témoignage sur les mentalités et le mode de vie: sur un territoire assez restreint, on compte plus de 550 villas, dont plus de 120 présentent un caractère monumental; elles ont été édifiées entre le 14e siècle et le milieu du 19e siècle, mais leur apogée se situe au cours du 16e siècle. Vivre dans une villa plutôt qu'en ville et se consacrer éventuellement à la production d'huile d'olive sélectionnée et de vins prisés devient maintenant non seulement un choix existentiel, mais aussi une forme intelligente d'investissement.

La province de Lucques englobe encore des paysages mineurs, ou moins connus, comme la région de la Garfagnana, avec ses grandes parois blanches de marbre, entamées par les carrières, qui de loin ont l'air de montagnes couvertes de neige. Ce sont les Alpes apuanes, qui ne ressemblent absolument pas à l'Apennin, mais plutôt aux Alpes, avec leurs pointes dénudées, leurs moraines très abruptes, leurs crêtes, leurs parois à pic. On peut

zen, die in ganz Europa gültig waren. Die Palazzi in der Stadt und die Villen auf den Hügeln bergen zahlreiche Kunstschätze, die die Öffentlichkeit jedoch nur selten zu sehen bekommt, da die Luccheser ungern Einblick in ihre Privatsphäre gewähren. Im Mittelalter suchte die papstfreundliche guelfische Stadt auch den Schutz des Kaisers und ging mit Genua ein Bündnis gegen die verhaßten Pisaner ein. Als Abschreckung für alle Feinde, auch die gefürchteten Florentiner, entstand zwischen dem 15. und 17. Jahrhundert die berühmte Befestigungsanlage. Dreißig Meter breite Erdwälle wurden mit zwölf Meter hohen Ziegelsteinmauern umgeben. Von dort aus blickt man auf die ganze Stadt, auf den mit Steineichen bepflanzten Turm des Palazzo Guinigi, die imposante Statue des Erzengels Michael auf der Schaufassade von San Michele in Foro, sowie auf den wie eine Spitzenarbeit durchbrochenen Glockenturm von San Frediano. Lucca ist ein herausragendes Beispiel für behutsame Stadtplanung. Die jüngeren Häuser des 18. und 19. Jahrhunderts fügen sich harmonisch in die mittelalterliche Stadtstruktur ein. »Es gab nie Zerstörungen, Invasionen oder sonstige traumatische Ereignisse«, erklärt die Schriftstellerin Francesca Duranti. »Die mächtige Befestigungsanlage ist vollständig erhalten. Sie war im Grunde nutzlos, denn sie mußte nie einem Angriff standhalten. Die Luccheser, reiche Kaufleute, Handwerker und Großgrundbesitzer, haben stets lieber bezahlt als gekämpft.«

Auch die Umgebung von Lucca ist reich an Sehenswürdigkeiten, wie beispielsweise die Kirche von Gattaiola, ein Juwel romanischer Baukunst. In Richtung Altopascio liegt Montecarlo, ein Dorf langobardischen Ursprungs, mit dem winzigen Teatro dei Rassicurati, einem Schmuckstück aus dem 18. Jahrhundert. In der Region Brancoleria finden sich zahlreiche alte Pfarrkirchen. Erwähnenswert ist natürlich auch der Kurort Bagni di Lucca, in dem sich schon der französische Schriftsteller Michel de Montaigne (1533–1592) und der deutsche Dichter Heinrich Heine aufhielten. Und dann gibt es noch die zahlreichen Villen, architektonische Kostbarkeiten, die für einen mondänen Lebensstil stehen. In einem recht überschaubaren Gebiet befinden sich

pénétrer profondément à l'intérieur de la chaîne qui longe la côte en empruntant les nombreuses routes et pistes créées pour accéder aux carrières de marbre. Ces dernières sont splendides en elles-mêmes, aussi bien lorsque de véritables cascades de roches marmoréennes se dressent en lançant des éclairs blancs, que lorsqu'on les entrevoit à travers les fentes de la roche.

En définitive, la Toscane constitue un havre de paix. Mais un mystère demeure: de quelle nature exacte est la fascination qu'elle a exercée et qu'elle continue d'exercer sur tant d'écrivains et d'artistes, sur tant d'hommes illustres du passé et d'hommes ordinaires du présent, sur les gens simples comme sur les êtres les plus sophistiqués? Est-elle due à sa nature paisible, à son climat, à son patrimoine artistique, aux efforts accomplis en vue de lui garantir un avenir meilleur, à la conscience de l'incroyable richesse dont dispose la région sur le plan architectural et culturel? Les illustrations de cet ouvrage se lisent comme autant de descriptions minutieuses et détaillées de la vie à l'intérieur des maisons et des palais d'hier et d'aujourd'hui. En Toscane, l'homme vit dans une étroite symbiose avec cette terre où il est né ou qu'il a choisie comme seconde patrie. Il semble même que son angoisse existentielle y trouve un apaisement – c'est notamment le cas pour le jeune héros des «Dernières Lettres de Jacopo Ortis» (1802) de l'écrivain romantique italien Ugo Foscolo. Ce qui était vrai autrefois l'est encore de nos jours pour ceux qui décideront de se rendre en Toscane, d'entreprendre ce «voyage au cœur de l'harmonie».

über 550 Anwesen, davon sind 120 monumentale Bauwerke. Sie entstanden zwischen dem 14. und der Mitte des 19. Jahrhunderts mit einer Blütezeit im 16. Jahrhundert. Wer heute der Stadt den Rücken kehrt und eine Villa erwirbt, um dort ausgewählte Öle und Weine zu erzeugen, entscheidet sich nicht nur für eine andere Lebensweise, sondern tätigt auch eine intelligente Investition.

In der Provinz Lucca gibt es Landstriche, die weniger bekannt sind. Dazu gehört die Garfagnana mit ihren imposanten Marmorsteinbrüchen, die aus der Ferne schneebedeckten Bergen gleichen. Dort beginnen die Apuanischen Alpen, die keine Gemeinsamkeiten mit dem Apennin aufweisen, sondern mit ihren nackten Gipfeln, extrem steilen Geröllfeldern, Gebirgskämmen und senkrechten Wänden eher alpinen Charakter haben. Auf den zahlreichen Straßen und Wegen, die für den Abtransport der Marmorblöcke angelegt wurden, kann man bis tief in diese parallel zur Küste verlaufende Gebirgskette eindringen. Hoch oben leuchtet das weiße Gestein, und man erhascht durch eine Felsspalte hindurch einen Blick auf die atemberaubend schönen Marmorbrüche.

Die Toskana ist ein Ort des Friedens mit einer geheimnisvollen Aura. Doch was genau macht nun den Zauber aus, den diese Region auf so viele Schriftsteller und Künstler von damals und heute ausübt, auf bedeutende Persönlichkeiten ebenso wie auf sogenannte »einfache Leute«? Vielleicht sind es Landschaft und Klima, vielleicht auch der Reichtum an Kunstwerken und historischen Traditionen oder auch das Bemühen um eine bessere Zukunft. Die Abbildungen dieses Buchs lesen sich wie eine Chronik. Jedes noch so kleine Detail kündet vom Geist, der die Palazzi und Häuser heute und gestern erfüllte. In der Toskana leben die Menschen im Einklang mit der Natur. Das gilt für die gebürtigen Toskaner ebenso wie für diejenigen, die hier ihre Wahlheimat gefunden haben. Hier löst sich jedweder existentielle Zweifel auf. Schon der hoffnungslose Held des romantischen Romans »Die letzten Briefe des Jacopo Ortis« (1802) von Ugo Foscolo machte diese Erfahrung – und auch heute erlebt dies noch jeder, der zu einer Reise in die Toskana aufbricht, einer »Reise in die Harmonie«.

Firenze e dintorni

Au 13e siècle, les Pucci habitaient déjà à l'endroit où se trouve au-jourd'hui le palais qui porte leur nom, à côté de la cathédrale de Flo-rence. D'après Giorgio Vasari (1511–1574), le célèbre historien de l'art florentin, le palais a été conçu au début du 16e siècle par l'architecte florentin Bartolomeo Ammannati, un contemporain de Michel-Ange. Récemment, l'édifice où vit la marquise Cristina Pucci a retrouvé un rôle dans la vie publique de la cité florentine: il sert de cadre aux acti-vités artisanales et commerciales liées à la maison Pucci. Par ailleurs, c'est ici que le marquis Emilio Pucci (1914–1992) a entrepris sa car-rière de styliste de mode, et ses extraordinaires dessins y sont amou-reusement conservés.

Palazzo Pucci

In the 13th century, the houses of the Pucci family huddled together near the Cathedral, where the palazzo named after them stands today. According to the famous Florentine art historian Giorgio Vasari (1511–1574), Palazzo Pucci itself was built in the early years of the 16th century, to a design by the Florentine architect Barto-lomeo Ammannati, a contemporary of Michelangelo. Recently, it has again started to play a role in the life of Florence. The internal spaces and original structure have been adapted to accomodate craft workshops and retail outlets. And it was here that Marquis Emilio Pucci (1914–1992) began his forays into the world of fashion. His extraordinary designs are lovingly conserved and displayed in the Palazzo Pucci – now the home of Marchioness Cristina Pucci.

In dem Adelspalast unmittelbar neben dem Florentiner Dom begann der Marchese Emilio Pucci (1914–1992) seine Karriere als internatio-nal erfolgreicher Modeschöpfer. Seine liebevoll restaurierten Zeich-nungen sind in einigen Räumen präsentiert. Der Palast wurde im 16. Jahrhundert errichtet, aber Archivaufzeichnungen belegen, daß die Familie Pucci schon im 13. Jahrhundert an dieser Stelle einige Häuser besaß. Laut dem berühmten florentinischen Kunsthistoriker Giorgio Vasari (1511–1574) stammt der Entwurf für den Palast von dem Florentiner Baumeister Bartolomeo Ammannati, einem Zeitge-nossen Michelangelos. Heute befinden sich in einigen der jahrhunder-tealten Räumlichkeiten Werkstätten und Geschäfte des Hauses Pucci. Außerdem residiert hier die Marchesa Cristina Pucci.

Tuscany Interiors   Palazzo Pucci

Double page précédente: Dans l'imposant corridor du deuxième étage se trouvent des fauteuils florentins du 17e siècle. Dans les vitrines qui datent de la même époque est disposée une collection de porcelaine de Meissen.
Page de gauche: Le mobilier vénitien de ce salon date de la première moitié du 18e siècle.
Ci-dessus: De dimensions relativement modestes, cette salle à manger est richement ornée d'une fresque attribuée à Luigi Ademollo (1764–1849). Le tapis de table date du 16e siècle.
A droite: le passage reliant la salle à manger et la cuisine.

Previous pages: Florentine chairs dating from the 17th century in the gallery on the second floor. The Florentine display cases contain services of Meissen porcelain.
Facing page: This drawing room was decorated in the Venetian style during the first half of the 18th century.
Above: Although this dining room is relatively small, it is richly decorated with a large fresco attributed to Luigi Ademollo (1764–1849). The cloth on the table dates from the 16th century.
Right: the passageway leading from the dining room to the kitchen.

Vorhergehende Doppelseite: In dem weitläufigen Korridor im zweiten Stock stehen prächtige florentinische Sessel aus dem 17. Jahrhundert. In den Vitrinen aus derselben Epoche befindet sich eine wertvolle Sammlung Meißener Porzellan.
Linke Seite: Die venezianische Einrichtung dieses Salons stammt aus der ersten Hälfte des 18. Jahrhunderts.
Oben: Dieser relativ kleine Speiseraum ist prachtvoll dekoriert mit einem Luigi Ademollo (1764–1849) zugeschriebenen Fresko. Die Tischdecke stammt noch aus dem 16. Jahrhundert.
Rechts: Dieser Durchgang verbindet das Speisezimmer mit der Küche.

Ci-dessus, à gauche: Une chambre comporte un lit à baldaquin luc-quois du 17e siècle.
Ci-dessus, à droite, et page de droite: Cette chambre de style Empire a été spécialement aménagée en 1805 pour Emilio Pucci, ancêtre de l'actuelle propriétaire et maire de Florence sous Napoléon.

Above left: a bedroom with a 17th-century, four-poster bed made in Lucca.
Above right and facing page: This bedroom was decorated in the Empire style in 1805 especially for Emilio Pucci, an ancestor of Cristina Pucci, who was Mayor of Florence under Napoleon.

Oben links: ein Schlafzimmer mit einem Luccheser Himmelbett aus dem 17. Jahrhundert.
Oben rechts und rechte Seite: ein Schlafzimmer im Empire-Stil. Es entstand 1805 für Emilio Pucci, einem Vorfahren der heutigen Besitzerin, der unter Napoleon Bürgermeister von Florenz war.

L'appartement florentin du critique littéraire Luigi Baldacci abrite une extraordinaire collection d'œuvres d'art. Tourné à l'origine vers le 17e siècle florentin, son intérêt s'est ensuite étendu à l'ensemble du baroque italien. Des éclairages subtils font surgir les tableaux et les objets de la pénombre. Cette collection, qui s'enrichit continuellement, traduit à la fois un impérieux besoin de possession, presque physique, et une sorte de recherche obsessionnelle de la perfection esthétique, tangible aussi bien au niveau de la combinaison des objets que des rapprochements chromatiques, du choix des fonds et des détails. Toute la richesse du baroque à son apogée est rassemblée dans cette demeure où les saintes en extase, les Enfants Jésus, les Madones polychromes et les animaux empaillés, témoins d'une époque fastueuse, retrouvent toute leur splendeur.

Luigi Baldacci

The flat in Florence where the literary critic Luigi Baldacci lives is also home to an astounding collection of artworks. The enigmatic half-light is here and there penetrated by shafts of radiance that illuminate paintings or spotlight "objets d'art". The collection has been built up gradually over many years by the owner in a search that at first focused on the Florentine 17th century and was later extended to include the rest of Italy. Baldacci continues to add to it in an almost obsessive quest for physical ownership and above all for perfection, in the compositions themselves, in their use of colour and in their detail and background. All the sumptuous richness of the triumphant high Baroque period can be appreciated in these rooms, where Saints in ecstasy and the Infant Jesus relive their splendour next to gaudy Madonnas and stuffed animals from an age that made a virtue of opulence.

In dem geheimnisvollen Halbdunkel seines Domizils hat der Literaturkritiker Luigi Baldacci eine Fülle von Kunstgegenständen versammelt. Hier und dort erhellt ein Lichtstrahl wertvolle Gemälde und hebt weich die Konturen wohlüberlegt arrangierter Skulpturen hervor. Baldacci ist fast besessen von dem Bedürfnis, Kunstwerke sein eigen zu nennen und ihnen ein perfektes Ambiente zu schaffen. So achtet er beim Arrangement der einzelnen Werke auf farbliche Harmonie sowie auf das Zusammenspiel von Vorder- und Hintergrund. Seine Leidenschaft gilt dem italienischen Barock mit Schwerpunkt auf Florenz. In Baldaccis »Wunderkammer« befinden sich neben religiösen Meisterwerken des Barocks, wie weiblichen Heiligen in Verzückung, Jesuskindern und Madonnen, auch ausgestopfte Tiere. Hier haben Zeugen einer prunkvollen Epoche ein neues glanzvolles Zuhause gefunden.

Double page précédente, à gauche: Luigi Baldacci devant la toile «Judith et Holopherne» de Cecco Bravo (1607–1661); deux bustes de saints polychromes napolitains flanquent une châsse vitrée abritant un Enfant Jésus.

Double page précédente, à droite: Une statue de sainte Thérèse d'Avila datant du 18e ou 19e siècle et deux chandeliers en bois patiné façon bronze sont disposés devant un grand tableau napolitain du 18e ou 19e siècle figurant saint Jérôme.

A droite: Une «Sainte Catherine» réalisée par Lorenzo Pasinelli (1629–1700) surmonte une collection d'oiseaux empaillés.

Ci-dessous: Au mur, on peut voir «La Lamentation sur le Christ mort» de Cecco Bravo. Au premier plan, on remarque deux Vierges et un Enfant Jésus napolitain du 18e ou 19e siècle.

Previous pages, left: Luigi Baldacci seated under the oil painting "Judith Slaying Holofernes" by Cecco Bravo (1607–1661); two Neapolitan painted busts of saints flank a display cabinet holding an Infant Jesus.

Previous pages, right: An imposing "Saint Jerome" painted in Naples during the 18th or 19th century provides the backdrop for a "Saint Theresa of Avila" dating from the same period and two bronze-patinated wood candlesticks.

Right: a collection of stuffed birds under a "Saint Catherine" by Lorenzo Pasinelli (1629–1700).

Below: "Lamentation Over the Dead Christ" by Cecco Bravo hangs on the wall. In the foreground are two Virgins and a Nativity-scene Infant Jesus made in Naples during the 18th or 19th century.

Vorhergehende Doppelseite, links: Luigi Baldacci vor dem Öl-gemälde »Judith ermordet Holofernes« von Cecco Bravo (1607–1661); zwei neapolitanische Heiligenbüsten wachen über die Skulptur des Jesuskindes.

Vorhergehende Doppelseite, rechts: Vor dem »Heiligen Hiero-nymus« aus der neapolitanischen Schule des 18./19. Jahrhunderts

richtet eine »Heilige Theresia von Avila« die Augen gen Himmel, flankiert von zwei mit Bronzepatina überzogenen Holzleuchtern.

Rechts: Eine Sammlung ausgestopfter Vögel ist unter dem Gemälde »Die Heilige Katharina« von Lorenzo Pasinelli (1629–1700) plaziert.

Unten: Vor der »Beweinung Christi« Cecco Bravos sieht man zwei Madonnen und ein Jesuskind aus einer neapolitanischen Krippe des 18./19. Jahrhunderts.

Ci-dessus: *Dans le salon, à côté de «La Vierge à l'Enfant» en bois polychrome, œuvre siennoise du 16e siècle, on distingue la «Sainte Madeleine» du peintre bergamasque Carlo Ceresa (1609–1679) et la «Bacchanale» de Cecco Bravo. Une grande urne chinoise trône au milieu d'autres vases. La lampe à huile votive en bronze date du 18e siècle.*
A droite: *Dans la salle à manger, une reproduction d'un buste du dessinateur de jardins André Le Nôtre, réalisée sous Napoléon III, est disposée entre deux chandeliers Louis XVI, devant un autre petit buste du 18e siècle.*

Above: *the living room. Behind the painted wooden "Virgin and Child", carved in Siena in the 16th century, are the paintings "Saint Magdalena" by the Bergamese artist Carlo Ceresa (1609–1679) and a "Baccanale" by Cecco Bravo. A huge Chinese urn stands out from the other vases; the bronze votive oil lamp dates from the 18th century.*
Right: *In the dining room, a Napoleon III reproduction of a bust of the French landscape gardener André Le Nôtre stands between two Louis XVI candlesticks in front of another small 18th-century bust.*

Oben: *Im kleinen Salon hängen rechts neben der bemalten sienesischen Holzskulptur »Madonna mit Kind« aus dem 16. Jahrhundert die Gemälde »Heilige Magdalena« des bergamaskischen Malers Carlo Ceresa (1609–1679) und »Bacchanal« von Cecco Bravo. Zwischen anderen Gefäßen steht eine große chinesische Vase unter einer bronzenen Votiv-Öllampe aus dem 18. Jahrhundert.*
Rechts: *Das Speisezimmer ziert ein Abguß einer Büste des französischen Gartenarchitekten André Le Nôtre aus der Zeit des Second Empire sowie eine weitere kleine Büste aus dem 18. Jahrhundert. Sie wird flankiert von Louis-Seize-Kerzenleuchtern.*

L'élégant Palazzo Antinori a gardé intacte sa belle apparence du 15e siècle. C'est l'un des palais toscans les plus achevés de cette époque. L'historien de l'architecture Alfredo Lensi l'a qualifié d'«unique en son genre, grâce à l'extraordinaire unité qui règne entre l'intérieur et l'extérieur, reflétant très fidèlement les caractéristiques essentielles de l'architecture civile de la Renaissance ». La parfaite harmonie du palais est mise en valeur par l'ameublement somptueux. Le moindre détail de la décoration a été pensé avec soin. Il y a quelques années, on a même effectué des recherches dans les archives et procédé à quelques réaménagements. Le palais est habité aujourd'hui par le marquis Piero Antinori et son épouse Francesca. Ils descendent de la famille, enrichie dans la sériciculture et le commerce de la soie, qui l'a acheté à la fin du 15e siècle.

Palazzo Antinori

Offering a superb visual impact that has remained unaltered since the 15th century, Palazzo Antinori is the best-proportioned example of a building of its kind in Tuscany. The architectural historian Alfredo Lensi called it "a unique construction of its type, with such harmony of interior and exterior that it conveys with an absolute immediacy the essential qualities of Renaissance domestic architecture." Every detail of the decoration is of stunning quality, thanks in part to the scholarly restoration work that was carried out a few years ago. Today, the family of the Marquis Piero Antinori and his wife Francesca live in the palazzo. Descendants of the family of silk-traders who purchased the building in the 15th century, they ensure by their presence that Palazzo Antinori will continue to delight the eye; its magnificent structure enhanced by the symmetries of its sumptuous furnishings.

Über fünfhundert Jahre hinweg hat sich der Palazzo Antinori seine Pracht unversehrt bewahrt. Edle Proportionen machen ihn zu einem der schönsten unter den toskanischen Palazzi der Renaissance – kein Wunder also, daß ihn der Architekturhistoriker Alfredo Lensi als »einzig in seiner Art« bezeichnete und sagte: »Die vollkommene Einheit zwischen innen und außen vermittelt sehr anschaulich die wesentlichen Qualitäten der Wohnhäuser der Renaissance.« Für die mit größter Sorgfalt und unter Berücksichtigung selbst kleinster Details ausgeführte Restaurierung wurden sogar alte Schriften und Archivdokumente herangezogen. Schließlich ist der prächtige Palazzo seit Ende des 15. Jahrhunderts im Besitz der Familie Antinori, die einst wertvolle Seidenstoffe nach ganz Europa lieferte. Derzeit bewohnen Marchese Pietro Antinori und seine Ehefrau Francesca die prachtvollen, geschmackvoll eingerichteten Innenräume.

Page précédente: une galerie au plafond à poutres apparentes. La statue «Matrona romana» d'époque romaine provient de la collection d'antiquités du Earl of Pembroke à Wilton House, et fut acquise par la famille Antinori avant la Seconde Guerre mondiale. Le pavement est en tomettes à incrustations de marbre.
Ci-dessus: le bureau-bibliothèque et son splendide bureau de notaire du 17e siècle. Le grand tableau qui représente la famille Pellegrini de Venise est dû au Tintoret.
A droite: un buffet surmonté d'un tableau de Agostino Tassi (vers 1566–1644) qui représente le mât de cocagne planté sur l'escalier du Capitole à Rome.

Previous page: the gallery, where the Roman statue "Roman Matron" dating from the 2nd century AD stands in attendance. It came from the collection of antiquities at Wilton House, seat of the Earl of Pembroke. The statues were acquired by the Antinori family before the Second World War. The ceiling is in wood beams and terracotta brick while the floor is in terracotta with marble inlays.
Above: The centrepiece of the library-cum-studio is a superb 17th-century notary's desk. The large painting of the Venetian Pellegrini family is by Tintoretto.
Right: a sideboard and a painting by Agostino Tassi (c. 1566–1644) of a greasy pole erected during public celebrations on the steps leading up to the Capitol in Rome.

Vorhergehende Seite: die Galerie mit der römischen Statue »Matrona romana«. Sie stammt ursprünglich aus der Antikensammlung des Earl of Pembroke in Wilton House und wurde von der Familie Antinori vor dem Zweiten Weltkrieg erworben. Bemerkenswert sind die massiven Deckenbalken und der Terrakotta-Fußboden mit Einlegearbeiten aus Marmor.

Oben: Ein besonders schöner Notarschreibtisch aus dem 17. Jahrhundert steht in dem Raum, der als Bibliothek und Arbeitszimmer dient. Das beeindruckende Porträt der venezianischen Familie Pellegrini stammt von Tintoretto.
Rechts: Das Gemälde von Agostino Tassi (um 1566–1644) über der Anrichte zeigt einen Festmast auf der Treppe zum römischen Kapitol.

A droite: une cheminée de pierre ornée d'un blason, deux vases et une statuette de majolique. Le tableau représente un gentilhomme du 17e siècle.
Ci-dessous: Les fenêtres donnent sur la façade baroque de l'église San Gaetano et, au fond, la cathédrale de Florence. La splendide tapisserie renforce l'aspect particulièrement lumineux de la pièce.

Right: detail of a stone fireplace bearing a family crest, two vases and a majolica statuette. The painting portrays a 17th-century gentleman.
Below: The window looks onto the Baroque façade of the church of San Gaetano against the background of the Florentine Cathedral. A magnificent tapestry provides a lustrous complement to the furnishings.

Rechts: Über den beiden Vasen und der Majolika-Statuette auf dem Kaminsims hängt das Porträt eines Edelmanns aus dem 17. Jahrhundert.
Unten: Vom Fenster aus sieht man die Barockfassade von San Gaetano und dahinter den Florentiner Dom. Der farbenprächtige Wandteppich verleiht dem Raum eine ganz besondere Leuchtkraft.

Sculpteur et peintre d'origine sicilienne, Alfio Rapisardi est florentin d'adoption. «La vie de l'artiste est vagabonde. Aujourd'hui, j'habite cette maison-atelier, dans le ‹centro storico› de Florence, mais demain je ne sais pas. Pour les artistes, Florence représente l'idéal absolu, une ville d'une beauté parfaite». Comme il vit et travaille dans les mêmes pièces, celles-ci changent continuellement d'aspect. Il est probable qu'aujourd'hui, dans la chambre, un nu de l'artiste polonais Johnny Malechisky n'est plus disposé au-dessus d'une main sculptée par l'artiste sicilien Angelo Badalà, d'une sculpture figurant un danseur venant de Thaïlande et d'un fossile âgé de deux millions d'années. De même dans le salon rouge, où une œuvre d'étudiant du maître de maison ne repose plus sur une colonne, et le dessin d'un élève anonyme de Salvador Dalí, accroché à la fausse porte, a été remplacé par des œuvres plus récentes.

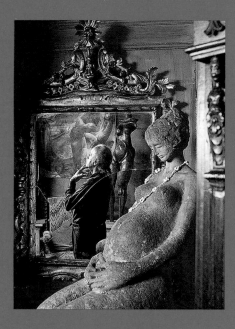

Alfio Rapisardi

Alfio Rapisardi, a sculptor and painter originally from Sicily, is a Florentine by adoption. "The artist's life is a nomadic one," he says. "Today I am living in this house right in the historic centre of Florence, but tomorrow who knows. For an artist, Florence is all you could wish for, a city whose beauty makes it perfect." Since Rapisardi lives and works in the same rooms, they are continually undergoing transformations. In the bedroom, the nude, drawn by the Polish artist Johnny Malechisky looks down, perhaps temporarily, on a hand sculpted by the Sicilian artist Angelo Badalà, a carving of a dancer from Thailand and a two-million-year-old fossil. In the red room as well, the formal study by Rapisardi mounted on a column might not be in the same position for much longer; and something more recent could well replace the work by an anonymous pupil of Salvador Dalí hanging on the imitation door.

Florenz ist die Wahlheimat des Bildhauers und Malers Alfio Rapisardi, der aus Sizilien stammt. »Wir Künstler«, so erklärt er, »führen ein Vagabundenleben. Heute lebe und arbeite ich hier, in diesem Haus im ›centro storico‹, dem historischen Zentrum. Was morgen sein wird, das weiß niemand. Für Künstler ist Florenz das Beste, was man sich wünschen kann, eine Stadt von makelloser Schönheit.« Die Wohnung des Künstlers verändert sich ständig, mit jedem seiner neuen Werke. Der Akt des polnischen Künstlers Johnny Malechisky befindet sich vermutlich schon nicht mehr im Schlafzimmer über der Skulptur einer Hand des sizilianischen Bildhauers Angelo Badalà, einem Tänzer aus Thailand und einem zwei Millionen Jahre alten Fossil. Und wahrscheinlich ersetzen bereits neuere Werke Rapisardis Akademiearbeit auf dem Pfeilerpodest ebenso wie die Zeichnung von einem unbekannten Schüler Salvador Dalís auf der gemalten Tür.

Ci-dessus: *Dans une pièce aux murs peints de couleur vive, les œuvres de l'artiste cohabitent avec un fauteuil du 17e siècle, aux accoudoirs sculptés, ainsi qu'avec un tabouret du 17e siècle revêtu de velours et un râtelier où sont rangés des hallebardes et des fusils. Le crâne utilisé comme modèle est un souvenir des années d'études.*
A droite: *Un angle intime de la maison abrite des sculptures érotiques et des cariatides réalisées par le maître de maison.*
Page de droite: *un lit à colonnettes torses et des tableaux d'amis.*

Above: *This brightly decorated room brings together the artist's own works, a 17th-century chair with carved, spiral arms, a 17th-century, velvet-upholstered stool and a rack of halberds and firearms. The skull, once used as a model for drawings, is a memento from the artist's student days.*
Right: *A corner of a room in the private part of the house with erotic sculptures and caryatids by the owner.*
Facing page: *Over the 17th-century bed with its spiral posts are hanging paintings by the artist's friends.*

Oben: *Lebhafte Farben beherrschen dieses Zimmer mit Werken des Hausherrn. Ein Sessel mit gedrechselten Armlehnen und ein samtbezogener Hocker – beide aus dem 17. Jahrhundert – flankieren einen Ständer mit Hellebarden und Gewehren. Der Totenschädel ist eine Erinnerung an die Lehrjahre in der Akademie und dient Rapisardi als Modell für Zeichnungen.*

Unten: *In einem Privatzimmer Rapisardis befinden sich erotische Skulpturen und Karyatiden des Künstlers.*
Rechte Seite: *Über dem Bett mit den gedrechselten Pfosten aus dem 17. Jahrhundert hängen Gemälde von Künstlerfreunden.*

L'architecte Giuseppe Chigiotti a restructuré cet édifice du quartier Santo Spirito à Florence, avec l'aide d'Alberto Morgando. Le bâtiment d'origine à vocation religieuse avait été transformé en une myriade de petits appartements. Les immenses pièces ont été redessinées en fonction de la trame des plafonds à caissons sans renoncer à la continuité spatiale. La maîtresse de maison se sent très bien dans cette demeure et aime recevoir des invités dans les pièces de facture moderne. Dans la salle de séjour, des meubles créés par Philippe Starck, Oscar Tusquets Blanca et Roberto Gerosa voisinent avec un tableau de l'artiste brésilienne Maria Cecilia Manuel Gismondi datant des années soixante. Dans la partie bureau, un guéridon en acajou du 19e siècle est disposé au-dessous d'une œuvre du peintre napolitain Giacomo Costa, réalisée en 1973

Vivere a Santo Spirito

In the Santo Spirito district of Florence, in a building that used to belong to a religious order before its conversion into tiny flats, the architect Giuseppe Chigiotti, assisted by Alberto Morgando, have successfully completed an impressive feat of rehabilitation. The spacious living spaces have been recreated in correspondence with caisson ceilings without sacrificing the continuity of the internal space. Above all, the owner loves the intimacy and privacy of the individual rooms. The spirit belongs to the past but the inspiration is very modern. The living area features contemporary items by Philippe Starck, Oscar Tusquets Blanca and Roberto Gerosa. On the wall hangs a painting from the Sixties by the Brazilian artist Maria Cecilia Manuel Gismondi. A 19th-century mahogany table is surmounted by a 1973 painting by Giacomo Costa from Naples.

Dieses Gebäude im Florentiner Stadtteil Santo Spirito restaurierte der Architekt Giuseppe Chigiotti gemeinsam mit Alberto Morgando mit viel Liebe zum Detail. Ursprünglich hatte es der Kirche gehört, bevor es in zahlreiche winzige Wohnungen aufgeteilt wurde. Bei der Umgestaltung griffen die Architekten auf moderne Materialien und Techniken zurück und rekonstruierten die ursprüngliche, großzügige Raumaufteilung anhand der Kassettendecken. Die alleinstehende Hausherrin empfängt gerne Gäste in ihrem modern eingerichteten Haus. Im Wohnraum stehen moderne Möbel von Philippe Starck, Oscar Tusquets Blanca und Roberto Gerosa. Dort hängt auch ein Gemälde der brasilianischen Künstlerin Maria Cecilia Manuel Gismondi aus den sechziger Jahren. Über dem kleinen Mahagonitisch aus dem 19. Jahrhundert im Büro befindet sich ein Gemälde des neapolitanischen Künstlers Giacomo Costa aus dem Jahr 1973.

Page de gauche: *l'espace repas. Sur la table Empire, on note un vase «Amazzonia» en polyuréthanne de Gaetano Pesce. Sur les petites tables basses «Cuginetto» créées par Enzo Mari, une sculpture d'Igor Mitoraj côtoie des céramiques des années quarante.*
Ci-dessus: *une salle de bain. Sur le guéridon original de Joseph Hoffmann (1870–1956) est posé un petit vase vénitien des années trente.*

Facing page: *the dining area. An "Amazzonia" vase in polyurethane by Gaetano Pesce stands on the Empire table. A sculpture by Igor Mitoraj and ceramics from the Forties adorn the "Cuginetto" side tables by Enzo Mari.*
Above: *a bathroom. A small Venetian vase from the Thirties stands on the original table designed by Joseph Hoffmann (1870–1956).*

Linke Seite: *die Eßecke. Auf dem Empire-Tisch steht die Polyurethan-Vase »Amazzonia« von Gaetano Pesce. Auf den »Cuginetto«-Tischchen von Enzo Mari befinden sich eine Skulptur von Igor Mitoraj sowie einige Keramikobjekte aus den vierziger Jahren.*
Oben: *Im Badezimmer steht ein Originaltischchen von Joseph Hoffmann (1870–1956) mit einer venezianischen Vase aus den dreißiger Jahren.*

Wanda Ferragamo avait dix-huit ans quand elle a franchi pour la première fois le seuil de cette imposante villa Renaissance. Elle venait
d'épouser Salvatore Ferragamo, le célèbre «bottier des stars», qui
rentrait en Italie après avoir vécu des années aux Etats-Unis. «Ma
première impression a été une sorte d'éblouissement, car le vestibule
donne directement sur une grande terrasse qui domine Florence». La
villa date du 16e siècle et il semble qu'elle ait appartenu à la famille
Strozzi, des banquiers florentins. Elle était déjà en partie meublée:
certains meubles d'origine n'avaient jamais été déplacés. «Naturelle-
ment, au cours des années, nous avons effectué un grand nombre de
modifications. Nos six enfants sont tous nés dans cette maison et j'ai
donc fait aménager neuf chambres à l'étage supérieur... Cette maison – ajoute-t-elle – est pleine de merveilleux souvenirs».

Wanda Ferragamo

Wanda Ferragamo was eighteen years old when she crossed the
threshold of this imposing Renaissance villa for the first time. She
was returning with her husband from their honeymoon. He, Salvatore Ferragamo, the celebrated "shoemaker of the stars", was himself coming home after spending many years in the United States.
"My first impression was of being surrounded by light," she recalls,
"because the entrance hall opens directly onto an immense terrace
with a view over Florence." The villa was built in the 16th century
and is thought to have belonged to the Strozzi family, famous
Florentine bankers. When the Ferragamos took possession, some
of the original furniture was still in place. "Of course we have made
many alterations over the years. Our six children were all born
here so I had the upper floor divided up into nine bedrooms. This
house," Wanda adds, "is full of wonderful memories."

Als frischgebackene Ehefrau trat Wanda im Alter von achtzehn Jahren
das erste Mal über die Schwelle der Renaissancevilla. Es war gleichzeitig der erste Schritt in ihr neues Leben mit Salvatore Ferragamo,
dem berühmten »Schuhmacher der Stars«, der aus den Vereinigten
Staaten nach Italien heimgekehrt war. »Ich war wie in Licht geba-
det«, erinnert sie sich noch heute an ihren ersten Eindruck. »Von der
großen Terrasse mit dem wundervollen Blick auf Florenz überflutete
helles Sonnenlicht die Eingangshalle.« Ursprünglich gehörte die Villa
aus dem 16. Jahrhundert wahrscheinlich der florentinischen Bankiers-
familie Strozzi. Sie war noch mit den Originalmöbeln eingerichtet.
»Aber natürlich«, erzählt Signora Ferragamo, »haben wir im Laufe
der Jahre vieles verändert. Unsere sechs Kinder sind hier geboren, und
deshalb habe ich das obere Stockwerk in neun Schlafräume aufteilen
lassen. Das ganze Haus steckt voll von schönen Erinnerungen.«

Page de gauche: *Wanda Ferragamo; un petit citronnier en pot; une fontaine ornée d'un putto dans le jardin.*
Ci-dessus: *La grande terrasse donne sur le jardin et domine Florence.*
A droite: *La villa Renaissance, où vit toujours Wanda, a été achetée par Salvatore Ferragamo en 1940.*

Facing page: *Wanda Ferragamo; a small, pot-grown lemon tree in the garden; a stone fountain decorated with a "putto", or small naked child.*
Above: *the splendid terrace that commands a superb view of the garden and Florence in the distance.*
Right: *The villa, built during the Renaissance, was purchased by Salvatore Ferragamo in 1940. Wanda still lives there.*

Linke Seite: *Wanda Ferragamo; ein Zitronenbäumchen; auf dem Brunnen im Garten vergnügt sich ein Putto.*
Oben: *Von der weitläufigen Terrasse an der Gartenseite der Villa hat man einen grandiosen Blick auf Florenz.*
Rechts: *In der Renaissancevilla, die Salvatore Ferragamo im Jahre 1940 erwarb, lebt Wanda noch heute.*

Ci-dessus: une pièce typique des villas florentines – le séjour servant également d'entrée – avec sa cheminée et l'escalier qui mène à l'étage supérieur.
A droite: détail montrant une pendule du 18e siècle et deux photos de Christian Dior.
Page de droite: La salle à manger au plafond à caissons et aux lambris sculptés abrite des meubles du 16e siècle, une tapisserie des Gobelins du 17e siècle et un lustre de Murano.

Above: a room typical of the villas in Florence. The living room, with its fireplace and wooden staircase leading to the upper floors, also serves as an entrance hall.
Right: detail of an 18th-century clock flanked by two photographs of the couturier Christian Dior.
Facing page: The sumptuous dining room has a caisson ceiling, carved woodwork, 16th-century furniture, a Gobelin tapestry made in the 17th century and a Murano chandelier.

Oben: In zahlreichen florentinischen Villen findet man einen solchen Wohnraum im Eingangsbereich des Hauses. Links sieht man einen Kamin und im Hintergrund die Holztreppe, die zu den oberen Stockwerken führt.
Rechts: eine Uhr aus dem 18. Jahrhundert und zwei Fotografien des Modezaren Christian Dior.
Rechte Seite: Das Speisezimmer mit Kassettendecke und geschnitzter Holzvertäfelung beherbergt Möbel aus dem 16. Jahrhundert, einen Gobelin aus dem 17. Jahrhundert und einen Leuchter aus Muranoglas.

Dans cette villa du vieux bourg de Settignano, au nord-est de Florence, l'atmosphère 19e siècle est toujours vivace. Les architectes se sont inspirés du tournant du siècle et de l'univers imaginaire du poète national Gabriele d'Annunzio qui voulait exalter les styles anciens. La villa présente une solide structure identique et se caractérise par une succession de pièces donnant sur un jardin aux allées dallées, agrémenté de statues, de vases et de tonnelles. L'intérieur offre un potpourri de styles historiques cher à l'éclectisme du 19e siècle, depuis l'austère Moyen Age en passant par le maniérisme du 16e siècle jusqu'au raffinement du 18e siècle. Des meubles originaux jouxtent des pastiches d'ancien, sans échapper à une légère influence de l'art nouveau qui dominait alors la scène européenne.

Una villa a Settignano

The ancient hamlet of Settignano lies to the north-east of Florence. In one of the villas there the "fin de siècle" lives on. Working at that time, the architects took their cues from the world of poet, author and master of rhetoric Gabriele d'Annunzio, who indeed wrote his major works in one of the neighbouring villas. D'Annunzio wanted the various styles of past centuries recalled to life. Solidly built, the villa boasts a series of rooms overlooking a garden, which is paved and decorated with statues, plant pots and a covered walk. The interior is a guided tour of the historical styles that appealed to the eclecticism of the last century, ranging from medieval austerity, through the Mannerism of the cinquecento to 18th-century elegance. Original pieces of furniture stand next to imitations that hark back to fashions of the past, including teasing hints at the Art Nouveau movement which was making its entry on the European stage as the villa was being built.

In dieser Villa in Settignano, im Nordosten von Florenz, ist das Fin de siècle noch lebendig. Zur Jahrhundertwende orientierten sich die Architekten an der Gedankenwelt des sprachgewaltigen Schriftstellers und Dichters Gabriele d'Annunzio, der das Wiederbeleben alter Stilformen forderte. Typisch für das Fin de siècle ist der kompakte Grundriß und die Zimmerfolge der Villen mit Blick auf den Garten, der Statuen, eine Gartenlaube und geplättelte Wege aufweist. Vor allem aber spiegeln auch die Innenräume den eklektizistischen Geist der Jahrhundertwende wider: von der Strenge des Mittelalters über den Manierismus des 16. Jahrhunderts bis zur Anmut des 18. Jahrhunderts. Neben Originalstücken finden sich auch Stilmöbel mit Anklängen an den Jugendstil, der zur Entstehungszeit der Villa Europa eroberte.

Double page précédente, à gauche: détail de la lucarne de la loggia vitrée avec la figure allégorique du Printemps.

Double page précédente, à droite: La terrasse donnant sur le jardin abrite une tonnelle et une statue de Pomone, déesse des fruits et des fleurs, œuvre des sculpteurs Bacci et Morandi, actifs dans la région au début du siècle.

Page de gauche: La loggia toscane classique est réinterprétée ici par l'insertion de vitraux polychromes. La table est la copie d'un modèle classique, selon l'usage du début du siècle. Les sièges sont des modèles originaux de Thonet. Au fond à droite, on remarque un télescope, à droite un haut porte-vase en rotin.

Ci-dessus: Le salon de musique évoque l'atmosphère de la Florence des 14e et 15e siècles, avec ses stalles de bois sculpté au fond et ses deux fauteuils au premier plan, réalisés par des artisans de la région d'après des modèles anciens.

Previous pages, left: detail of the skylight in the glass-fronted loggia with an allegorical portrait of spring.

Previous pages, right: The terrace overlooking the garden features a statue of Pomona, the goddess of fruit and flowers, by the sculptors Bacci and Morandi, who worked in the area in the early years of the 20th century.

Facing page: The loggia is in the classic Tuscan style, with the addition of coloured glass windows. The table is modelled on an antique design, as was the fashion in the early 20th century. The Thonet chairs are original. In the background there is a telescope on the left and a wicker flower-holder on the right.

Above: The atmosphere in the music room evokes 14th- or 15th-century Florence. The two chairs were made by local craft workers in the early years of the 20th century who were reproducing original models. In the background, a carved wood choir stall.

Vorhergehende Doppelseite, links: eine Allegorie des Frühlings im Oberlicht der verglasten Loggia.

Vorhergehende Doppelseite, rechts: Von der Terrasse blickt man in den Garten. Die Statue der Pomona, der Göttin der Früchte und Blumen, stammt von den Bildhauern Bacci und Morandi, die Anfang des Jahrhunderts in der Region tätig waren.

Linke Seite: Farbige Glasfenster schließen die klassische toskanische Loggia. Thonet-Stühle gruppieren sich um den Tisch, der – wie es zu Beginn des Jahrhunderts üblich war – klassischen Vorbildern nachempfunden ist. Im Hintergrund stehen ein Teleskop und ein Blumenständer aus Weidengeflecht.

Oben: Beim Betreten des Musikzimmers mit dem holzgeschnitzten Chorgestühl fühlt man sich in das Florenz des 14. und 15. Jahrhunderts zurückversetzt. Die Stühle sind zu Beginn des 20. Jahrhunderts von ortsansässigen Handwerken nach alten Modellen angefertigt worden.

Ci-dessus: *La chambre à coucher pastiche le style du 18e siècle. L'atmosphère feutrée, les coloris délicats, les décorations sont assortis aux peintures murales. Le tout a été réalisé par des artisans des environs au début du siècle. La décoration des meubles et des murs est due à un peintre nommé Cecchi.*

Above: *The bedroom is a tribute to the 18th century. The gracious, welcoming atmosphere, delicate colours and carefully matched décor eloquently evoke a bygone age. Everything was made by local craft workers in the early years of the 20th century. The furniture and walls were decorated by a painter named Cecchi.*

Oben: *Auch das Schlafzimmer ist mit Möbeln ausgestattet, die zu Beginn des 20. Jahrhunderts lokale Handwerker anfertigten. Es ist eine Hommage an die Vergangenheit: Weiche Formen, zarte Farben und auf die Wandmalereien abgestimmte Dekorationen waren kennzeichnend für das 18. Jahrhundert. Die Dekorationen der Möbel und Wände stammen von dem Maler Cecchi.*

Ci-dessus: *La salle de bains de la chambre d'amis est entièrement recouverte de précieux marbres polychromes aux tons gris et verts disposés de manière à former des dessins.*

Above: *The bathroom in the guest suite is decorated thoughout with solid marble in shades of grey and green. The sections have been carefully arranged into patterns.*

Oben: *Das Badezimmer des Gästeappartements ist vollständig mit kostbarem, zwischen Grau- und Grüntönen changierendem Marmor ausgekleidet. Die einzelnen Platten sind zu Mustern zusammengesetzt.*

La Villa Mandri, dans les environs de Reggello, présente la structure caractéristique des résidences des Médicis au début du 18e siècle. La façade donnant sur la vallée est encadrée par le profil puissant des tours. Au centre, un portique ombrage l'entrée et soutient une terrasse. Outre sa valeur historique et artistique, elle possède ce charme inimitable que confère l'usure du temps. Aujourd'hui la Villa Mandri est la résidence de l'antiquaire florentin Giovanni Pratesi, mais au fil des siècles, elle a souvent changé de propriétaire; elle a même parfois servi de résidence à des voyageurs sans racines, dont l'esprit des lieux a aussi conservé l'empreinte. Les meubles semblent être depuis toujours à la même place, de même que la tonnelle de glycine et le billard, dans la salle ornée de fresques inspirées d'Herculanum. L'atmosphère paraît éminemment littéraire, comme si l'on s'aventurait entre les pages d'un livre de l'écrivain Henry James.

Villa Mandri

Villa Mandri, near Reggello, is typical of the Medici residences built in the early 18th century. The main façade is surmounted by turrets and punctuated by a portico. Quite apart from its historical and artistic significance, Villa Mandri has an indefinable allure of its own conferred by that most subtle of decorative artists, the passage of time. Now owned by Florentine antique dealer Giovanni Pratesi, it has changed hands many times over the centuries and has offered hospitality to countless travellers who have left their invisible mark on its atmosphere. The interior has remained unchanged for many decades, as have the venerable wisteria-clad pergola and the billiard table in the room whose décor was inspired by Herculaneum. Any one detail could have been placed by an unseen hand into a scene from a Henry James' novel – set forever in the timeless world of Literature.

Die Villa Mandri bei Reggello ähnelt mit ihrer typischen, von Türmen flankierten Fassade den Medici-Villen vom Anfang des 18. Jahrhunderts. Doch neben ihrer architektonischen Bedeutung strahlt die Villa, die heute dem florentinischen Antiquitätenhändler Giovanni Pratesi gehört, eine ganz eigene Faszination aus, denn sie verdeutlicht den unaufhaltsamen Lauf der Zeit. Durch den von einem Bogengang beschatteten Eingang traten in den vergangenen Jahrhunderten zahllose Besitzer. Sie glichen rastlosen Reisenden, die hier nur kurz verweilten, dennoch aber ihre unverkennbaren Spuren hinterließen und diejenigen ihrer Vorgänger respektierten. So hat vieles seit jeher seinen festen Platz: die alte, von Glyzinien überwucherte Pergola ebenso wie der Billardtisch in dem mit wunderschönen, an Herculaneum erinnernden Wandmalereien verzierten Zimmer. Man fühlt sich versetzt in die Welt des Schriftstellers Henry James – als sei die Villa in dessen Büchern verewigt worden.

Page précédente: *la salle du billard, au plafond à caissons peints, avec son lustre et son paravent chinois dissimulant une cheminée sur laquelle est posée une horloge française du 18e siècle. Les décorations murales du 18e siècle s'inspirent de celles d'Herculanum.*

Page de gauche: *Le buffet de la salle à manger est surmonté par les armes des Médicis. La table, les sièges et les consoles datent du 19e siècle, de même que le lustre de style flamand.*

Ci-dessus: *Le salon central du premier étage de la villa, où subsistent des éléments anciens comme les sièges de pierre aménagés dans les profondes embrasures des fenêtres, possède un mobilier de la fin du 19e siècle. Deux vases Wedgwood posés sur des colonnes encadrent la cheminée toscane surmontée d'un miroir. Le lustre en bronze doré à pendeloques de cristal du 19e siècle est d'origine toscane.*

Previous page: *The billiard room has a painted caisson ceiling, a chandelier and a Chinese screen masking the fireplace. An 18th-century French clock adorns the mantelpiece and the decorations on the walls, inspired by those discovered at Herculaneum, also date from the 18th century.*

Facing page: *a dresser surmounted by the Medici coat of arms in one of the dining rooms. Dining table, chairs and console table are all 19th century, as is the Flemish-style chandelier.*

Above: *the main reception room on the first floor of the villa. Ancient elements such as the stone seats in the background have survived alongside the late 19th-century furniture. The Tuscan fireplace is surmounted by a mirror and flanked by two Wedgwood vases on supporting columns. The gilt-bronze chandelier ornamented with pendant drops was made in Tuscany and dates from the 19th century.*

Vorhergehende Seite: *Die Fresken aus dem 18. Jahrhundert im Billardzimmer entstanden nach dem Vorbild der Wandmalereien von Herculaneum. Vor dem Kamin steht ein chinesischer Paravent, auf dem Sims eine französische Uhr aus dem 18. Jahrhundert. Von der bemalten Kassettendecke hängt ein auffälliger Leuchter aus dem späten 19. Jahrhundert.*

Linke Seite: *Das Wappen der Medici bekrönt die Anrichte in einem der Speisezimmer. Die Ausstattung – Tisch, Stühle, Konsoltisch und flämischer Leuchter – stammt aus dem 19. Jahrhundert.*

Oben: *Der zentral gelegene Salon im ersten Geschoß ist im Stil des späten 19. Jahrhunderts eingerichtet. An dem toskanischen Lüster aus vergoldeter Bronze hängen Kristalltropfen. Zwei Wedgwood-Vasen auf Säulenpodesten flankieren den toskanischen Kamin, auf dessen Sims ein Wandspiegel steht. In den Fensternischen befinden sich noch die originalen Steinsitzbänke.*

Ci-dessus: *la chambre avec un lit à baldaquin du 18e siècle. Sur le mur du fond, on peut voir une grande broderie chinoise sur soie, au-dessus de la table de style néoclassique toscan comme les trois fauteuils.*
Page de droite: *la chapelle privée construite au 19e siècle. Le grand tableau accroché au mur appartient à l'école florentine du 18e siècle. Le vitrail de droite, en pâte de verre colorée, est orné du blason des Médicis.*

Above: *the bedroom with an 18th-century tester bed. A large Chinese silk embroidery decorates the far wall. The neoclassical Tuscan table is discreetly complemented by two chairs and an armchair.*
Facing page: *the chapel, which was built in the 19th century. The imposing painting on the wall is by the Florentine School of the 18th century. The stained-glass window on the right bears the Medici arms.*

Oben: *das Schlafzimmer mit einem Himmelbett aus dem 18. Jahrhundert. Im Hintergrund hängt eine großformatige chinesische Seidenstickerei. Der toskanische Tisch sowie die beiden Armstühle und der Sessel sind klassizistisch.*
Rechte Seite: *die im 19. Jahrhundert errichtete Familienkapelle. Das Gemälde über dem Altar schuf ein Florentiner Maler im 18. Jahrhundert. Das farbige Glasfenster rechts zeigt das Wappen der Medici.*

«L'architecture toscane est compacte et symétrique, il émane des maisons une sensation de mystère et de silence, comme dans les tableaux de Giorgio de Chirico» explique le célèbre architecte-designer italien Ettore Sottsass. En collaboration avec les architectes Marco Zanini et Mike Ryan, il a conçu une villa entre Florence et Pise qui respecte la tradition architecturale toscane. C'est un cube de deux étages revêtu de pierre blanche, avec un toit à double pente en aluminium rouge et quelques rares fenêtres. Le rez-de-chaussée comporte un vaste séjour-patio, autour de l'escalier, et une cuisine «à la toscane»; le premier étage abrite trois chambres. En outre une chambre d'amis aménagée dans les combles donne sur la terrasse. Toute la maison est bâtie autour d'un puits lumineux protégé par le toit en saillie, qui fournit un éclairage naturel indirect et diffus.

Una villa di Ettore Sottsass

According to Ettore Sottsass, a famous Italian designer and architect, who designed this villa between Florence and Pisa, there are times when traditions have to be respected. "Tuscan architecture is compact and symmetrical," he observes, "and the houses have a sense of mystery and silence, like the paintings of Giorgio de Chirico." The villa, designed with the architects Marco Zanini and Mike Ryan, is a white stone-clad cube built on two floors with a red aluminium pitched roof and few windows. The ground floor is the day area. The living room, arranged like a patio round the staircase, features a two-level ceiling as well as a Tuscan-style kitchen. There are three bedrooms on the first floor, and a fourth, in the attic overlooking the terrace, is set aside for guests. The focal point of the house is the light well, which is protected by the overhanging roof and enables daylight to reach all the rooms, providing a suffused, natural illumination.

»Die toskanischen Häuser scheinen unergründliche Geheimnisse zu bergen. Sie sind von fast unheimlicher Stille und erinnern an die magischen Gemälde von Giorgio de Chirico«, sagt der bekannte italienische Architekt und Designer Ettore Sottsass. Er entwarf gemeinsam mit den Architekten Marco Zanini und Mike Ryan zwischen Florenz und Pisa eine außergewöhnliche Villa, die auf moderne Weise die Bautradition der Toskana respektiert. Es entstand ein zweistöckiges, würfelförmiges Gebäude aus hellem Stein mit einigen wenigen Fenstern. Indirektes Licht erhalten die Räume durch eine das Gebäude oben umlaufende, verglaste Maueröffnung, die von dem vorspringenden Satteldach aus rotem Aluminium geschützt wird. Im Erdgeschoß ist um die Treppe herum der Wohnbereich angelegt, der durch die doppelte Raumhöhe wie ein Innenhof wirkt. Auch die Küche »alla toscana« liegt im Erdgeschoß. Im ersten Stock befinden sich drei Schlafzimmer. Unter dem Dach liegt das Gästeschlafzimmer, von dem man auf die Terrasse blickt.

Tuscany Interiors   Una villa di Ettore Sottsass

Double page précédente, à gauche: la porte de derrière, donnant sur le jardin.
Double page précédente, à droite: l'escalier qui part du premier étage et mène à la terrasse; la villa vue de loin.
Page de gauche: les escaliers qui donnent accès à la terrasse et aux chambres du premier étage.
Ci-dessus: la cuisine, avec un meuble conçu spécialement par Ettore Sottsass.

Previous pages, left: the entrance at the rear from the garden.
Previous pages, right: the staircase leading from the first floor to the terrace; a view of the villa from a distance.
Facing page: the main staircase going up to the terrace and the stairs that lead off to the first-floor bedrooms.
Above: the kitchen. The unit was designed by Ettore Sottsass.

Vorhergehende Doppelseite, links: der Hintereingang vom Garten aus gesehen.
Vorhergehende Doppelseite, rechts: eine steile Treppe führt vom ersten Stock hinauf zur Terrasse; Gesamtansicht der Villa.
Linke Seite: Die steile Rampe führt zur Terrasse, die Treppe in den ersten Stock.
Oben: die Küche. Der Schrank wurde nach einem Entwurf von Ettore Sottsass gefertigt.

Tuscany Interiors   Una villa di Ettore Sottsass

Page de gauche: Dans le séjour au pavement de tomettes, une division de granit forme un angle où l'on peut voir un meuble combinant des bois différents, conçu par Ettore Sottsass. La «Vierge à l'Enfant» de l'école romaine date de la fin du 17e siècle.
Ci-dessus, à gauche: une chambre à coucher avec un lit dessiné par Ettore Sottsass. Au mur, une lithographie du peintre futuriste Giacomo Balla (1871–1958).
Ci-dessus, à droite: Dans une autre chambre, on aperçoit un lit et un meuble d'angle dessinés par Ettore Sottsass. La lampe «Tolomeo» a été conçue par Michele de Lucchi.

Facing page: one corner of the living room. The floor is tiled in terracotta, the half-wall is in granite and the cupboard units and shelving in wood of various kinds were designed by Ettore Sottsass. The late 17th-century "Madonna and Child" is a painting of the Roman School.
Above left: a bedroom with a bed by Ettore Sottsass. The lithograph is by the futurist painter Giacomo Balla (1871–1958).
Above right: another bedroom with a bed and a corner unit designed by Ettore Sottsass. The "Tolomeo" lamp is by Michele De Lucchi.

Linke Seite: eine Ecke des fast sakral wirkenden Wohnzimmers mit einer halbhohen Wand aus Granit. Das Möbelstück aus verschiedenen Hölzern entwarf Ettore Sottsass. Die »Madonna mit Kind« ist das Werk eines römischen Malers vom Ende des 17. Jahrhundert. Der Fußboden ist mit Terrakotta gefliest.
Oben links: ein Schlafzimmer mit einem Bett von Ettore Sottsass. Darüber hängt eine Lithographie des futuristischen Malers Giacomo Balla (1871–1958).
Oben rechts: ein weiteres Schlafzimmer mit einem von Ettore Sottsass entworfenen Bett und Eckregal. Als Leselampe dient das Modell »Tolomeo« von Michele de Lucchi.

On raconte que la Villa di Granaiolo a été construite sur les ruines d'un ancien fort. Quoi qu'il en soit, les Pucci étaient implantés dans le Val d'Elsa dès le 13e siècle. Participant aux guerres civiles de l'époque, ils en ont subi les aléas: après avoir été exilés, ils purent ensuite récupérer leurs biens. La construction de la villa, qui appartient à la famille Pucci depuis 1600, remonte à la fin du 14e siècle. De nombreux personnages illustres y ont séjourné jusqu'à nos jours. En 1968, le marquis Emilio Pucci a chargé l'architecte Gae Aulenti de redessiner la partie sud du jardin: une pelouse et de grands degrés de pierre confèrent à l'édifice une dimension géométrique et un surcroît de majesté. Facile d'accès depuis Florence, la villa sert aujourd'hui de maison de campagne à la marquise Cristina Pucci.

Villa di Granaiolo

It is rumoured that Villa di Granaiolo is built on the ruins of an ancient fort. Whatever the truth of the matter, the Pucci family had already settled in Val d'Elsa in the 13th century. It was an age of civil strife and rapidly changing fortunes, and the Puccis too were involved; first being forced into exile and then restored to their estates. Villa di Granaiolo was built at the end of the 14th century. Over the years, many illustrious guests have stayed at the villa, which has belonged to the Puccis since 1600. In 1968, Marquis Emilio Pucci commissioned the architect Gae Aulenti to redesign part of the garden to the south with a lawn and flights of stone steps, which gave space and a sense of geometry to the villa itself and left the woods in their natural state. Today Villa di Granaiolo, which can be reached easily from Florence, is used by Marchioness Cristina Pucci as a country residence.

Vermutlich wurde die Villa di Granaiolo auf den Ruinen einer alten Burg errichtet. Jedenfalls tobten im 13. Jahrhundert im Val d'Elsa, dem Elsatal, heftige Kriege zwischen den verfeindeten Adelsfamilien. Auch die Puccis waren darin verwickelt und wurden erst verbannt, später aber wieder in ihre Ämter eingesetzt. Seit 1600 ist die herrschaftliche Villa aus dem späten 14. Jahrhundert in ihrem Besitz. Hier waren zahlreiche bedeutende Persönlichkeiten zu Gast und sind es auch heute noch. Die Wiese und die steinernen Stufen an der Südseite wurden 1968 von der Stararchitektin Gae Aulenti angelegt. Sie bringen die geometrische Formensprache des großzügigen Gebäudes perfekt zur Geltung. Unberührt blieb hingegen der hinter dem Anwesen liegende Wald. Heute dient die Villa mit den prachtvoll ausgestatteten Innenräumen der Marchesa Cristina Pucci als Landsitz.

Double page précédente, à droite: le salon d'accès, avec au mur les emblèmes de la famille Pucci et au sol un magnifique tapis dessiné par le marquis Emilio Pucci.

Page de gauche: Un fragment de sculpture romaine, posé sur le sol, cohabite avec une table baroque et des fauteuils Renaissance. Une magnifique corne d'abondance du 17e siècle en fer forgé orne le mur de cette salle de passage.

Ci-dessus: La grande cheminée supporte une belle collection de majoliques. Autour d'elle, on peut noter un coussin damassé, un fauteuil en bois et des urnes antiques.

A droite: un fauteuil florentin placé devant une magnifique tapisserie du 17e siècle.

Previous pages, right: the entrance hall with its family crests and the magnificent carpet designed by Marquis Emilio Pucci.

Facing page: A Roman sculpture has found a new home next to a Baroque table, Renaissance chairs and a magnificent wrought-iron, 17th-century cornucopia hanging on the wall of this connecting room.

Above: A damask cushion, a wooden chair and ancient urns are disposed in this room. A fine collection of majolica adorns the mantelpiece over the great fireplace.

Right: a Florentine chair against the backdrop of a superb, 17th-century tapestry.

Vorhergehende Doppelseite, rechts: der Empfangssalon mit den Familienwappen und einem prachtvollen, von Marchese Emilio Pucci entworfenen Teppich.

Linke Seite: Eine römische Skulptur, ein Barocktisch und Renaissance-Sitzmöbel bilden ein eindrucksvolles Ensemble in einem Durchgangszimmer. Die Wand ziert ein wunderschönes schmiedeeisernes Füllhorn aus dem 17. Jahrhundert.

Oben: Ein Sitzkissen aus Damaststoff, ein Holzstuhl und zwei antike Urnen sind in diesem Raum zu sehen. Den Sims des imposanten Kamins schmückt eine Majolika-Sammlung.

Rechts: ein florentinischer Stuhl vor einem Bildteppich aus dem 17. Jahrhundert.

Page de gauche: L'aspect sévère de la bibliothèque est adouci par le blanc des parois et du mobilier. Les photographies représentent des parents et des membres de la famille royale italienne. Des gravures du 18e siècle décorent les murs.
Ci-dessus: vue d'ensemble de la bibliothèque; au premier plan, un magnifique lutrin de la Renaissance; le tapis a été dessiné par le marquis Emilio Pucci.
A droite: détail d'une bibliothèque renfermant un dessin du marquis Emilio Pucci.

Facing page: The austere atmosphere of the library is relieved by the white of the walls and bookcases. Some of the photographs portray Puccis and the others are of members of the royal family. The small square frames contain 18th-century prints.
Above: a general view of the library with a stupendous Renaissance lectern in the foreground. The carpet was designed by Marquis Emilio Pucci.
Right: detail of one of the bookcases. The drawing is by Marquis Emilio Pucci.

Linke Seite: Das Weiß der Wände und Bücherschränke läßt die strenge Bibliothek lichter wirken. Die Fotos zeigen Angehörige der Familie und des italienischen Königshauses. An der Wand hängen Drucke aus dem 18. Jahrhundert.
Oben: Ansicht der Bibliothek. Im Vordergrund steht ein prächtiges Renaissance-Lesepult. Der Teppich entstand nach einem Entwurf von Emilio Pucci.
Rechts: Detail eines Bücherschranks mit einer von Marchese Emilio Pucci signierten Zeichnung.

Juchée sur les pentes de l'Apennin de Pistoia, cette villa en forme de petit château fort a été édifiée durant la première moitié du 19e siècle par un personnage fantasque, un certain Niccolò Puccini, surnommé le Bossu. Baptisée fort à propos La Forteresse, elle est entourée d'un vaste jardin paysager qui recèle des buis taillés en forme de pyramides et de boules, des statues, des inscriptions gravées, un temple de Pythagore et un Panthéon. La famille qui habite La Fortezza apprécie cet étonnant chef-d'œuvre de l'éclectisme, issu de l'esprit romantique et libertaire du siècle dernier. Cette reconstitution néogothique est chargée de symboles: on peut voir dans le vestibule les effigies de Pier Capponi et de Filippo Strozzi, deux personnages très significatifs de l'histoire de la Toscane, qui ont mené l'opposition républicaine contre les Médicis à la fin du 15e siècle.

Villa La Fortezza

Child of the boundless imagination of Niccolò Puccini, the extraordinary aristocrat known as "the Hunchback" who built it in the mid-19th century in the foothills of the Apennines near Pistoia, this curious embattled castle glories in the highly appropriate name of Villa La Fortezza. It is surrounded by a landscape garden whose box trees the topiarist's art has shaped into pyramids and spheres, and by statues, epigraphs and other buildings resembling the temple of Pythagoras and the Pantheon. The present owners appreciate life in the midst of the villa's unrestrained eclecticism and the romantic libertarian spirit that also inspired so many other captivating neo-Gothic follies all over Europe. Note, in the magnificently sumptuous entrance hall, the busts of Filippo Strozzi and Pier Capponi, who were leaders of the Republican opposition to the Medici at the end of the 15th century.

Die Villa La Fortezza erhebt sich wie eine alte Festung an den Hängen des Pistoieser Apennins. Tatsächlich wurde die kleine Burg aber in der ersten Hälfte des 19. Jahrhunderts von Niccolò Puccini, genannt der Bucklige, errichtet. Der als merkwürdig verschriene Aristokrat ließ bei dem Bau seiner ungewöhnlichen Phantasie freien Lauf. Zwischen kunstvoll beschnittenem Buchsbaum überraschen in dem weitläufigen Garten ein Pythagoras-Tempel und ein Pantheon. Die heutigen Besitzer der Villa La Fortezza schätzen das eklektizistische Gebäude, in dem der Geist der Romantik und die Freiheitsbestrebungen lebendig geblieben sind, die in Europa zu einer spektakulären Wiedererweckung der Gotik führten. Eine Anspielung auf jene Epoche findet sich in der prächtigen Eingangshalle mit den Büsten von Filippo Strozzi und Pier Capponi – Leitfiguren des Kampfes gegen die Tyrannenherrschaft der Medici im späten 15. Jahrhundert.

Page de gauche: un chapiteau orné du buste de Filippo Strozzi (1428–1491); un angle du jardin aux buis taillés en forme de sphère et de cône.
Ci-dessus: le château néogothique implanté au cœur du jardin.
A droite et double page suivante: La fantaisie exubérante néogothique éclate dans l'entrée, avec ses arcs en ogive, ses marqueteries de marbre, ses colonnes géminées et ses mosaïques.

Left page: a capital incorporating a bust of Filippo Strozzi (1428–1491); the topiarist's art has transformed box trees into spheres and cones.
Above: The neo-Gothic castle stands in the middle of the garden.
Right and following pages: Neo-Gothic fantasy has run wild in the entrance, where exuberant ogival arches, marble inlays, double columns and mosaic all jostle for attention.

Linke Seite: ein Kapitell mit der Büste von Filippo Strozzi (1428–1491); kegel- und kugelförmig beschnittener Buchsbaum im Garten.
Oben: Die neugotische Burg ist in eine weitläufige Gartenanlage eingebettet.
Rechts und folgende Doppelseite: Exzessive neugotische Fantasien beherrschen die Eingangshalle: Spitzbögen, Marmorinkrustationen, Doppelsäulen und Mosaikarbeiten.

FILIPPO STROZZI

PIER CAPPONI

Chianti

Le cinéaste italien Bernardo Bertolucci aurait pu s'inspirer de cette «fattoria» de rêve pour son film «Beauté volée». D'ailleurs, on retrouve dans l'argument du film la façon dont Matthew et Maro Spender vivent en terre toscane. Elle est en effet caractéristique de celle de nombreux étrangers, surtout des Anglais, venus s'installer dans cette région que l'on surnomme parfois le «Chiantishire». Le sculpteur et son épouse vivent depuis la fin des années soixante à San Sano, avec leurs enfants, dans cette ferme du 18e siècle. Ils produisent du vin, cultivent des légumes et fabriquent eux-mêmes leurs meubles. Mais ils trouvent également le temps de sculpter, de peindre et de dessiner. L'art fait partie intrinsèque de leur vie. En effet, Matthew est le fils du poète anglais Sir Stephen Spender et sa femme Maro la fille d'Arshile Gorky, peintre américain d'origine arménienne.

Matthew e Maro Spender

This idyllic "fattoria", an 18th-century farmhouse, served Italian director Bernardo Bertolucci as the model for the house in his film "Stealing Beauty". The life led by the owners Matthew and Maro Spender is typical of that led by the many foreigners, particularly those from England, who have chosen to settle in Tuscany, affectionately known as "Chiantishire". Matthew, a well-known sculptor, is the son of the English poet Sir Stephen Spender, while his wife Maro is the daughter of the "émigré" Armenian painter Arshile Gorky. Both like to think of themselves as Bohemians, living the way all true artists used to live. Since the late Sixties, they have been bringing up their children and making their own wine on their 18th-century farm at San Sano. They till the soil, grow flowers and vegetables, and make furniture by hand. Of course, they also find time for sculpture, painting and drawing.

Diese idyllische »fattoria«, ein Gutshof aus dem 18. Jahrhundert, hätte dem italienischen Regisseur Bernardo Bertolucci als Vorbild für das Haus in seinem Film »Gefühl und Verführung« dienen können. Auch das Leben, das die Besitzer Matthew und Maro Spender führen, findet sich in Bertoluccis Schilderungen wieder. Es ist typisch für die vielen, insbesondere englischen Aussteiger, die in der Toskana, vor allem im sogenannten »Chiantishire«, ihr Domizil haben. Der Bildhauer und seine Frau leben seit den späten sechziger Jahren hier in San Sano. Sie ziehen ihre Kinder groß, bauen ihren eigenen Wein an, ernten auf den Feldern Gemüse und schreinern sogar ihre Möbel selbst. Aber sie finden auch Zeit zu bildhauern, zu malen und zu zeichnen. Die Kunst liegt ihnen im Blut, denn Matthews Vater ist der englische Schriftsteller Sir Stephen Spender, während Maro die Tochter des armenisch-amerikanischen Malers Arshile Gorky ist.

Double page précédente, à gauche: *la ferme des époux Spender; la table pour déjeuner sous la pergola.*

Double page précédente, à droite: *Matthew Spender au travail dans son atelier, au milieu de ses sculptures.*

Page de gauche: *Les deux jarres disposées au pied de l'escalier sinusoïdal contiennent l'une du sel, l'autre du sucre. La sculpture féminine en terre cuite est l'œuvre de Matthew. Le «Ganymède chevauchant l'aigle» de style art nouveau, dans l'angle de l'escalier, est le cadeau d'un antiquaire. Le lustre florentin en fer forgé a été déniché dans un marché aux puces de Florence et repeint par Maro.*

Ci-dessus: *Un curieux lustre réalisé par Matthew surmonte la table de la salle à manger, à côté de la grande cheminée.*

Previous pages, left: *the Spenders' "fattoria"; the table where the couple enjoy alfresco luncheons under the pergola.*

Previous pages, right: *Matthew Spender at work surrounded by his sculptures.*

Facing page: *One of the jars next to the steep, twisting staircase holds salt and the other sugar. The female terracotta figure is Matthew's work. In the corner, halfway up the stairs, there is an Art Nouveau "Ganymede Mounted on an Eagle", which was a gift from an antiquarian. The Florentine wrought-iron chandelier was picked up at a second-hand market in Florence and repainted by Maro.*

Above: *An unusual chandelier that Matthew made hangs over the dining table next to the imposing fireplace.*

Vorhergehende Doppelseite, links: *die »fattoria« des Ehepaars Spender; der Tisch lädt zum Essen unter der Pergola ein.*

Vorhergehende Doppelseite, rechts: *Matthew Spender bei der Arbeit in seinem Atelier.*

Linke Seite: *Die beiden Gefäße neben der geschwungenen Treppe enthalten Salz und Zucker. Die weibliche Terrakotta-Skulptur ist ein Werk von Matthew. Ein Antiquitätenhändler schenkte den Spenders die Jugendstilskulptur »Ganymed auf dem Adler« in der Ecke an der Treppe. Den ortstypischen schmiedeeisernen Leuchter, den Maro neu bemalt hat, haben die Spenders auf einem Flohmarkt in Florenz entdeckt.*

Oben: *Über dem Eßtisch vor dem imposanten Kamin hängt eine eigenwillige Lampe von Matthew.*

Page de gauche: La cuisine comporte de vieux meubles, comme la table en bois de cyprès et les chaises cannées, trouvées chez un antiquaire. Toutes les majoliques et les céramiques décorées, bols, assiettes, compotiers, ainsi que les carreaux qui ornent les parois, sont l'œuvre de Maro.
Ci-dessus: un détail de la cuisine. Le tableau placé sous l'horloge est une mosaïque réalisée par la marraine de Maro, l'artiste américaine Jeanne Reynald. La tête de marbre est une œuvre de Matthew.
A droite: un simple évier de pierre ancien.

Facing page: The kitchen is furnished with old pieces, such as the cypress table and the wicker chairs that the couple acquired from an antiquarian. Maro made all the decorated majolica and ceramics, including the bowls, plates, fruit bowls and the tiles.
Above: detail of the kitchen. All the decorated pottery and majolica was made by Maro. The picture under the kitchen clock is a mosaic portrait of Maro's godmother, the American artist Jeanne Reynald. The marble head is Matthew's work.
Right: the old plain stone sink.

Linke Seite: Den Tisch aus Zypressenholz und die Bambusstühle in der gemütlichen Küche fanden die Spenders bei einem Antiquitätenhändler. Die zahlreichen Majolika- und Keramikarbeiten – Schüsseln, Teller, Obstschalen und sogar Kacheln – fertigte Maro selbst.
Oben: Ansicht der Küche. Das Mosaikporträt unter der Uhr ist ein Geschenk von Maros Patentante, der amerikanischen Künstlerin Jeanne Reynald. Der Marmorkopf ist ein Werk von Matthew.
Rechts: ein schlichtes, altes Steinbecken.

Ci-dessus: Le lit et l'armoire ont été fabriqués par Matthew et décorés par Maro.
Page de droite: la salle de bains. La baignoire placée au centre divise la pièce en deux. Tous les tableaux ont été réalisés par Maro et ses deux filles, alors que la tête posée sur le rebord de la fenêtre est de Matthew, comme le water-closet surélevé et doté d'un rangement, à gauche, dont la forme s'inspire du trône papal de la cathédrale d'Anagni. Le lustre est en cristal de Bohême. Le vieux plafond aux poutres apparentes a été restauré et peint en bleu.

Above: bedroom furniture hand-made by Matthew and hand-decorated by Maro.
Facing page: the bathroom. The tub positioned in the centre of the room creates two distinct spaces. All of the pictures were executed by Maro or her daughters. The head in the window on the right is by Matthew, who also made the raised lavatory and cupboard unit on the left, inspired by the shape of the papal throne in the cathedral of Anagni. The chandelier is in Bohemian glass and the original beamed ceiling has been restored and painted blue.

Oben: Matthew schreinerte Bett und Schrank, Maro verzierte sie anschließend.
Rechte Seite: Die freistehende Wanne unterteilt das Badezimmer. Sämtliche Gemälde stammen von Maro und ihren beiden Töchtern, während Matthew die Büste auf der rechten Fensterbank schuf. Zu der erhöhten Toilette mit integriertem Stauraum inspirierte ihn der Papstthron in der Kathedrale von Anagni. Von der Decke mit den restaurierten, blau gestrichenen Balken hängt ein böhmischer Kristalleuchter.

Villa Vignamaggio

The approach to Villa Vignamaggio, an estate of some hundred
hectares of vineyards and olive groves, is from Panzano near Greve
in Chianti, along the "Vecchia Chiantigiana" road. The villa was originally built in the 15th century but took on its present aspect about
a century later when a new wing, which today houses the cellars,
was added. Villa Vignamaggio is known also as Villa Gherardini
after the family of the former owners. Some historians believe that
it was a member of the Gherardini family, Lisa (born in the villa in
1479), whose portrait was painted by Leonardo da Vinci. What is
certain is that da Vinci stayed at Villa Gherardini for a short time
before abandoning Tuscany for Milan in 1506; and it may have
been against the backdrop of these hills that the artist painted the
world's most famous canvas, the portrait of a lady with an in-
scrutably enigmatic smile.

Tuscany Interiors   Villa Vignamaggio

Double page précédente, à gauche: une statue du 18e siècle placée dans une niche à l'arrière de la villa.

Double page précédente, à droite: quatre aperçus évocateurs de portes et de passages faisant communiquer les cours.

Ci-dessus, à gauche: un passage menant à la bibliothèque. On remarque un petit portique à colonnes et un tapis persan aux motifs circulaires assez inhabituels.

Ci-dessus, à droite: une chambre à coucher au plafond voûté, avec un baldaquin en tissu du 17e siècle fixé au mur, qui se trouvait déjà dans la villa à l'arrivée du propriétaire actuel. On peut noter un lustre de Murano.

Page de droite: la salle à manger, dans la partie la plus ancienne de la villa, avec son plafond aux voûtes en calotte. Autour de la table en bois massif sont disposés des sièges toscans traditionnels. Le tableau qui orne le mur du fond est l'œuvre d'un artiste napolitain anonyme du 17e siècle. Le lustre d'argent provient également du sud de l'Italie. A gauche, sous la fenêtre, on remarque un siège de pierre caractéristique de la Toscane.

Previous pages, left: An 18th-century statue can be seen in a niche at the rear of the villa.

Previous pages, right: four details of door and passageways in the courtyards.

Above left: a passageway to the library. Note the colonnaded porch and the oriental rug with its unusual circular pattern.

Above right: a bedroom with vaulted ceiling and an 18th-century wall-mounted fabric tester, which the present owner found in the villa when he acquired it. The chandelier is in Murano glass.

Facing page: The dining room in the oldest part of the villa has a sail-vaulted ceiling and a solid-wood table, around which are arranged traditional Tuscan dining chairs. The painting on the far wall is by an anonymous 17th-century Neapolitan artist. The silver candelabrum also originates from the south of Italy. In the background on the left, a typical Tuscan stone seat can be observed under the window.

Vorhergehende Doppelseite, links: eine Nische an der Rückseite der Villa mit einer Statue aus dem 18. Jahrhundert.

Vorhergehende Doppelseite, rechts: vier malerische Ansichten von Türen in den Innenhöfen und Hofdurchgängen.

Oben links: der Durchgang zur Bibliothek. Auffallend sind der von Säulen getragene Portikus und der Orientteppich mit den ungewöhnlichen Kreismustern.

Oben rechts: Im Schlafzimmer mit der Gewölbedecke befindet sich ein Himmelbett, dessen Stoffbaldachin noch aus dem 18. Jahrhundert stammt. Der heutige Eigentümer fand ihn bereits in der Villa vor. Von der Decke hängt ein Murano-Leuchter.

Rechte Seite: Im ältesten Teil des Hauses liegt das Speisezimmer mit der Gewölbedecke mit Stichkappen. Um den Tisch aus Massivholz gruppieren sich toskanische Stühle. Das Gemälde im Hintergrund stammt von einem unbekannten neapolitanischen Maler des 17. Jahrhunderts. Auch der Silberleuchter ist süditalienischer Herkunft. Links in der Fensternische befindet sich eine für die Toskana typische Steinsitzbank.

Cette ferme isolée sert depuis de longues années de refuge, hiver comme été, à une famille qui apprécie les vacances toutes simples, dans un cadre rustique. Au milieu d'une campagne splendide, c'est l'endroit idéal pour contempler des aurores et des couchers de soleil magnifiques dans le silence recueilli de la nature. Les oliviers et les vignes fournissent l'huile et le vin que l'on consomme avec les amis qui vivent dans les environs. Le bois touffu qui couvre une partie de la propriété contribue à la douceur du climat. Seuls quelques travaux de restauration indispensables ont été effectués, pour entretenir les structures de la demeure, retrouver son style d'origine et conserver les éléments préexistants, comme les poutres des plafonds ou les encadrements des portes et fenêtres. Les meubles viennent de la région.

Podere La Casina

This farmhouse is the traditional refuge in summer and winter of the family that purchased the property many years ago. Lovers of the simple life, they take refuge in this rustic hideaway with its splendid views of the surrounding countryside, where the sun climbs and descends in the silent splendour of a natural environment. Around them grow the olive trees and vines that yield the oil and wine they share with the many friends they have made in the area. Part of the estate has been left as woodland, which helps to keep the climate cool in the summer and mild in winter. Only a few essential alterations have been made to the property but with the avowed intention of maintaining the structure and style of the building and conserving the features that were already there, such as the beams of the ceilings and the door and window fittings. All the furniture is made locally.

Abgeschieden und still liegt das Landgut La Casina in der herrlichen Hügellandschaft unweit von Siena. Hier lassen sich atemberaubende Sonnenaufgänge und -untergänge erleben. Seit vielen Jahren genießt die Familie der Besitzer das einfache, ländliche Leben auf dem »podere«. Sie bauen ihren eigenen Wein und auch Oliven an, die sie dann gemeinsam mit den neu gewonnenen Freunden aus der Nachbarschaft kosten. Im Sommer wie im Winter sorgt der nahegelegene dichte Wald für ein angenehmes Klima. Die einfühlsame Restaurierung konzentrierte sich auf das Wesentliche: die ursprünglichen Strukturen, der Stil des Gebäudes sowie die Deckenbalken, Tür- und Fenstereinfassungen sollten erhalten bleiben. Selbst die Möbel stammen aus der Umgebung.

Double page précédente, à gauche: *Un vase contenant des roses est posé sur le rebord d'une fenêtre.*
Double page précédente, à droite: *Podere La Casina; le bois proche vu par l'embrasure d'une fenêtre.*
Ci-dessus: *L'entrée comporte un sommier recouvert de tissu, une table et des sièges toscans ainsi que des appliques en terre cuite.*

Previous pages, left: *a vase of roses on a window-ledge.*
Previous pages, right: *Podere La Casina; a view of the nearby woods from one of the windows.*
Above: *The intimate entrance is furnished with a table and chairs in the Tuscan style, a cloth-upholstered divan bed and terracotta wall lamps.*

Vorhergehende Doppelseite, links: *ein Glas mit Rosen auf einer Fensterbank.*
Vorhergehende Doppelseite, rechts: *Podere La Casina; durch ein Fenster blickt man auf den nahegelegenen Wald.*
Oben: *Im gemütlichen Eingangsbereich stehen ein kissenbedecktes Sofa, ein toskanischer Tisch und Stühle. Die Wandleuchten sind aus Terrakotta.*

A droite: un banc dans l'entrée, surmonté de chapeaux de paille.
Ci-dessous: une chambre d'amis au matelas et aux coussins recouverts de «mezzeri», des toiles de coton imprimé traditionnelles.
Double page suivante: la cuisine avec ses meubles et ses plats toscans et siciliens.

Right: straw hats hanging above a bench in the entrance.
Below: a guest room. The mattress and cushions are upholstered with "mezzeri", traditional printed cloth.
Following pages: The kitchen is full of furniture and crockery from Tuscany and Sicily.

Rechts: Über einer Bank im Eingangsbereich hängen Strohhüte.
Unten: ein Gästezimmer. Matratze und Kissen sind mit »mezzeri« überzogen, traditionell bedruckter Walkfilz.
Folgende Doppelseite: Die Küche ist mit Möbeln und Keramik aus der Toskana und Sizilien ausgestattet.

Le chianti que nous connaissons aujourd'hui doit sa fortune au baron Bettino Ricasoli (1809–1880), expert en agronomie et éminent politicien. Il mit au point le procédé de production du chianti dans son cellier du Château de Brolio, en établissant vers 1850 la proportion des différents cépages qui le composent. Ce procédé a été conservé jusqu'à nos jours et donne au chianti ce goût si caractéristique. Après diverses vicissitudes, la famille Ricasoli a recouvré la propriété des chais; c'est le baron Francesco qui s'en occupe. Le château rouge, perché sur une colline, fut profondément remanié au 19e siècle dans le style néogothique siennois. Il est encore habité durant l'été par le père de Francesco, prénommé Bettino comme son illustre arrière-grand-père, qui participa activement au «Risorgimento», à l'unification de l'Italie.

Castello di Brolio

The wines of Chianti owe their international fame and fortune to Baron Bettino Ricasoli (1809–1880), an expert on farming matters as well as a celebrated statesman. It was in his cellars at the Castello di Brolio around 1850 that the Chianti winemaking technique was perfected, and the proportions still used in the blend of grapes were laid down. The technique is observed to this day, and gives Chianti its unmistakable freshness of flavour. After a somewhat chequered period in its history, the cellar is once again owned by the family, with Baron Francesco Ricasoli in charge. Inside the red hilltop castle is a veritable warren of rooms, many of which were decorated in the 19th century in the Sienese neo-Gothic style. It is still the summer home of Francesco's father, Bettino, great-grandson of the other Bettino Ricasoli who contributed so much to the "Risorgimento", the unification of Italy.

Dem einflußreichen Großgrundbesitzer und Politiker Baron Bettino Ricasoli (1809–1880) hat das inzwischen weltbekannte Weinbaugebiet Chianti unendlich viel zu verdanken. Der kundige Baron experimentierte in den Kellern seines Castello di Brolio mit der Chianti-Herstellung, bis er um 1850 das ideale Mengenverhältnis der Rebsorten fand. Dieses gilt auch heute noch und verleiht dem Chianti seinen unverkennbaren, frischen Geschmack. Nach einer wechselvollen Geschichte ist die Traditionskellerei wieder im Besitz der Ricasoli und wird von Baron Francesco geleitet. Die rote, malerisch auf einer Anhöhe gelegene Burg verfügt über ungezählte, prachtvolle Innenräume, die im 19. Jahrhundert im Stil der sienesischen Neugotik restauriert worden sind. Die Sommermonate verbringt hier gewöhnlich Francescos Vater Bettino, ein Urenkel jenes Politikers, der eine wichtige Rolle im »Risorgimento«, der Einigung Italiens, spielte.

Double page précédente, à gauche: des fenêtres géminées couvertes de plantes grimpantes; détail du salon, avec une armure et une fresque évocatrice.

Double page précédente, à droite: La grande salle à manger à l'imposante table en bois massif a été décorée au 19e siècle conformément au goût néogothique alors à la mode.

Ci-dessus, à gauche: Ce corridor unit les deux salons du «piano nobile», du premier étage.

Ci-dessus, à droite: La chambre à coucher du 15e siècle aux voûtes en calotte, surnommée la «chambre verte», n'a pas été modifiée par la rénovation du 19e siècle.

Page de droite: le vestibule, vu du salon. Une tapisserie aux armes de la famille Ricasoli surmonte la commode toscane.

Previous pages, left: a mullioned window peeks through the exuberant foliage of the climbing plants; a detail of a suit of armour and an attractive fresco in the main reception room.

Previous pages, right: The focus of attention in the dining room is the enormous, solid-wood dining table carved in the neo-Gothic style in vogue when it was made during the last century.

Above left: A corridor connects the two reception rooms on the "piano nobile" or main floor.

Above right: The domical-vaulted 15th-century bedroom known as the "Green Room" was unaffected by the restructuring carried out in the 19th century.

Facing page: the entrance hall seen from the main staircase. A tapestry bearing the Ricasoli family crest hangs over a locally made antique wooden chest.

Vorhergehende Doppelseite, links: ein Zwillingsfenster mit Überfangbogen versteckt sich hinter Kletterpflanzen; Teilansicht des Salons mit einer Rüstung und einem Fresko.

Vorhergehende Doppelseite, rechts: Der riesige Tisch aus massivem Holz bildet den Mittelpunkt des Speisesaals, der im Stil der Neugotik ausgestattet ist.

Oben links: Der Korridor verbindet die beiden Salons im »piano nobile«, dem Hauptgeschoß.

Oben rechts: das Schlafzimmer mit Kuppelgewölben aus dem 15. Jahrhundert. Das sogenannte »grüne Zimmer« blieb unberührt von den Umbauten im 19. Jahrhundert.

Rechte Seite: Blick von der großen Treppe auf die Eingangshalle. Über der toskanischen Truhe hängt ein Wandteppich mit dem Wappen der Familie Ricasoli.

Double page précédente: L'immense salon au plafond en bois à caissons et aux murs tendus de cuir de Cordoue, regorge de tapis, d'élégants divans et d'une ornementation foisonnante de style néo-gothique.

Ci-dessus: Le vieux chianti, le meilleur, mûrit en fûts de chêne. Le chianti jeune est présenté dans des «fiaschi», des bouteilles au long col caractéristique, enveloppées de paillons.

A droite: Le Château de Brolio, entouré d'un puissant bastion défensif, est attribué à l'architecte florentin Giuliano da Sangallo (vers 1445–1516).

Previous pages: the immense, wooden-ceilinged drawing room. The walls are covered in Cordoba leather, rugs overlap on the floor and the elegant sofas stand resplendent amid the profuse neo-Gothic decoration.

Above: Chianti matures in oak casks. Young Chianti is filled into "fiaschi", long-necked, broad-bellied bottles wrapped in straw.

Right: the castle surrounded by the daunting defensive ramparts attributed to the Florentine architect Giuliano da Sangallo (c. 1445–1516).

Vorhergehende Doppelseite: Die Wände des riesigen Salons mit Holzkassettendecke sind mit Cordobaleder bezogen. Der Salon besticht durch seine zahllosen Teppiche, eleganten Sofas und die reichhaltige neugotische Ausstattung.

Oben: Der Chianti reift in Eichenfässern. Junger Chianti wird in »fiaschi« abgefüllt, bauchige, strohumwickelte Flaschen mit langem Hals.

Rechts: Die mächtige Befestigungsmauer des Castello di Brolio wird dem florentinischen Baumeister Giuliano da Sangallo (um 1445–1516) zugeschrieben.

A droite: *le jardin à l'italienne aménagé à la base du bastion sud.*
Ci-dessous: *vue des chais qui s'étendent sur des kilomètres au pied du Château de Brolio.*

Right: *the Italian garden in the shadow of the south-facing rampart.*
Below: *the cellars that extend for kilometres underneath the Castello di Brolio.*

Rechts: *der italienische Garten am Fuß der südlichen Befestigungsmauer.*
Unten: *Die Weinkeller unter dem Castello di Brolio erstrecken sich über mehrere Kilometer.*

Siena e le Crete

Palazzo d'Elci

The origins of Palazzo d'Elci, which overlooks the Campo, date back to Etruscan times. The building formed part of the city walls until the year 1300. Much of the furniture and the interior decoration, as it appears today, are by the Sienese architect Agostino Fantastici (1782–1849). "We have a duty to enjoy the beauty of this house," claims Countess Cesarina Pannocchieschi d'Elci, who lives in Palazzo d'Elci with her son, Andrea. Since the year 982 it had been a residence of knights, ambassadors and cardinals, and, consequently, the sumptuous rooms had, in the countess's view, acquired the atmosphere of a museum. That was why she decided to rearrange the furniture and do some restoration work. "It was like a breath of fresh air," she says, "and I'm going to leave my mark on the house, just as my forebears did."

Double page précédente, à gauche: le comte Andrea Pannocchieschi d'Elci et sa fiancée Marina Gennari; détail de la décoration: des tentures d'Agostino Fantastici disposées au-dessus d'une porte du salon.

Double page précédente, à droite: l'angle d'une pièce donnant sur le Campo, la place principale de Sienne, et la célèbre Torre del Mangia. La table en marqueterie date du 18e siècle comme le petit tableau au cadre octogonal; le portrait d'homme est attribué à Georges de La Tour (1593–1652). Le palais est situé dans la «Contrada dell'Oca», le quartier de l'Oie, qui participe avec succès au Palio, la célèbre course de chevaux qui a lieu deux fois par an sur le Campo. Le grand-père d'Andrea a été capitaine de l'équipe pendant dix-huit ans et son père Vieri pendant vingt ans; il a gagné deux fois avec son cheval nommé Salomé.

Ci-dessus: un salon dit «di passo» ou «de passage». Les deux fauteuils de style Empire ont été fabriqués à Sienne; la console et le miroir sont de style Louis XVI. A gauche, un tableau de Rutilio Manetti (1571–1639) surmonte un meuble marqueté du 18e siècle.

Page de droite: un détail du «salone giallo», le salon jaune, qui sert de chambre d'hôtes et qui a été décoré en 1899. Le grand portrait représente un membre de la famille Pannocchieschi qui fut ambassadeur en Espagne.

Previous pages, left: Count Andrea Pannocchieschi d'Elci and his fiancée, Marina Gennari; detail of the drape decoration by Agostino Fantastici over a door in one of the reception rooms.

Previous pages, right: the corner of a room looking onto the Campo with a view of the Torre del Mangia. The inlaid table dates from the 18th century, as does the painting in the small octagonal frame. The portrait is attributed to Georges de La Tour (1593–1652). Palazzo d'Elci stands in the "Contrada dell'Oca", the "Goose district" of the city, which takes part in the Palio horse race held twice a year in the Campo. Andrea's grandfather was the Captain of the Contrada dell'Oca team for eighteen years and his father, Vieri, led it for a further twenty; twice winning the Palio with his horse Salomé.

Above: a "di passo", or walk-through, reception room. The two chairs were made locally in the Empire style. The console table and the mirror are Louis Seize; on the left, over the 18th-century inlaid cabinet, is a painting by Rutilio Manetti (1571–1639).

Facing page: detail of the "salone giallo", the Yellow Room, which is used as a guest room. It was decorated in 1899. The large portrait is of a Pannocchieschi who served as ambassador to Spain.

Vorhergehende Doppelseite, links: Andrea Pannocchieschi d'Elci mit seiner Verlobten Marina Gennari; Detail der Innenausstattung mit Vorhängen von Agostino Fantastici über der Tür eines Salons.

Vorhergehende Doppelseite, rechts: Durch das Fenster dieses Zimmers blickt man auf die Torre del Mangia. Der zierliche Tisch mit Einlegearbeiten und das Gemälde in achteckigem Rahmen stammen aus dem 18. Jahrhundert. Das Porträt eines Mannes wird Georges de La Tour (1593–1652) zugeschrieben. Der Palazzo d'Elci gehört zur »Contrada dell'Oca«, der Contrade der Gans, eine der Nachbarschaftsgemeinschaften Sienas, die am zweimal jährlich stattfindenden »Palio«, dem bekannten Pferderennen auf der Piazza del Campo, teilnehmen. Andreas Großvater war für achtzehn Jahre, sein Vater Vieri für zwanzig Jahre »Capitano« der Contrade. Vieris Pferd Salomé verhalf der »Contrada dell'Oca« zweimal zum Sieg.

Oben: ein »Salotto di passo«, ein kleiner Durchgangssalon mit zwei sienesischen Empire-Stühlen. An der hinteren Wand finden sich ein Konsoltisch und ein Spiegel im Louis-Seize-Stil. Links hängt über der Kommode mit Intarsienarbeiten aus dem 18. Jahrhundert ein Gemälde von Rutilio Manetti (1571–1639).

Rechte Seite: Teilansicht des »salone giallo«, des Gelben Salons, der als Gästezimmer genutzt wird. Das imposante Gemälde zeigt einen Vorfahren der Pannocchieschi, der Gesandter am spanischen Hof war. Die Dekorationen stammen aus dem Jahre 1899.

Ci-dessus: La décoration du salon rouge a été exécutée en 1859 à
l'occasion du mariage d'Achille Pannocchieschi d'Elci et d'Elena Pucci.
Page de droite: la salle à manger. La vaisselle de porcelaine à décor
floral a été réalisée par la manufacture Richard Ginori en 1756. La
comtesse a l'habitude de la laver personnellement à la main.
Double page suivante: une chambre à coucher.

Above: The Red Room was decorated on the occasion of the marriage
of Achille Pannocchieschi d'Elci to Elena Pucci in 1859.
Facing page: the dining-room. The table is laid with floral-patterned
porcelain, made by Manifattura Richard Ginori in 1756, that the
countess insists on washing by hand herself.
Following pages: a bedroom.

Oben: Der Rote Salon entstand 1859 anläßlich der Hochzeit von
Achille Pannocchieschi und Elena Pucci.
Rechte Seite: das Speisezimmer. Das wertvolle Porzellanservice mit
Blumendekor von 1756 aus der Manufaktur Richard Ginori spült die
Contessa persönlich mit der Hand.
Folgende Doppelseite: ein Schlafzimmer.

Un jeune médecin célibataire vit dans ce logement aménagé dans un groupe de «case a torre», des maisons médiévales, adossées à la muraille. Il bénéficie d'une vue superbe sur la campagne et de la proximité du centre historique de Sienne. L'appartement est formé d'une ancienne salle au plafond peint à poutres apparentes et de deux autres pièces contiguës prises sur une maison voisine. L'architecte Giuseppe Chigiotti a donc dû procéder à une restructuration minutieuse et ardue. Il a fallu abattre des divisions internes ajoutées au cours du temps. L'essentiel, aux yeux du jeune médecin, était d'économiser l'espace pour disposer d'un grand séjour. C'est pour cette raison que l'on a construit la mezzanine originale de la chambre à coucher, destinée à servir de penderie, avec son escalier aux demi-marches de hauteur alternée. Le mobilier contemporain en bois clair est délibérément discret.

Una casa a torre

The young doctor who lives in this flat is a bachelor. He has made his home in part of a group of "case a torre" (tower houses), built against the medieval walls of Siena. Here, he enjoys both a wonderful view of the surrounding countryside and the convenience of being close to the "centro storico". The choice was a shrewd one but it meant that the architect Giuseppe Chigiotti had to employ great skill and care in converting the property. The flat comprises a main room with a painted-beam ceiling and two smaller rooms in the adjoining building. Partitions had been inserted by previous residents but the new owner removed them since he wanted to have as much living space as possible at his disposal. A logical consequence was the entresol in the bedroom with its flight of high stairs to provide wardrobe space. The modern wood furniture in pale shades is informal and deliberately understated.

Lichte Räume mit modernen, schlichten Möbeln aus hellem Holz — so stellte sich der junge, alleinstehende Arzt seine Wohnung vor. Diese Vorgabe war eine Herausforderung für den Architekten Giuseppe Chigiotti, denn die Wohnung befindet sich in einem Komplex von ineinander verschachtelten »case a torre«, mittelalterliche Turmbauten, die sich unmittelbar an der Befestigungsmauer von Siena befinden. Zwei der Räume mit den original bemalten Deckenbalken gehörten ursprünglich zu einem anderen Gebäude, so daß die Trennwände neu gesetzt werden mußten. Mit großem Ideenreichtum gewann Chigiotti zusätzlichen Raum. So zog er etwa im Schlafzimmer einen Hängeboden für einen Ankleideraum ein, der über eine originelle Treppe erreicht wird. Er verwirklichte einen Traum: modernes Wohnen mit Blick auf die wundervolle Umgebung von Siena und gleichzeitiger Nähe zum weltbekannten »centro storico«.

Double page précédente, à gauche: l'ensemble de «case a torre» (l'appartement se trouve dans la maison du milieu).
Double page précédente, à droite: l'escalier aux demi-marches de hauteur alternée de la chambre. Il mène à la mezzanine aménagée au-dessus de la salle de bain, et qui sert de penderie. Les lumières murales, tamisées par une dalle de verre, ont été conçues par Giuseppe Chigiotti.
Page de gauche: le séjour. Sur la desserte d'Alvar Aalto, on remarque l'arrosoir de la collection «Milano», créé par Riccardo Dalisi. Les petits fauteuils sont signés Thonet. Au fond, à côté du fauteuil «Bergère» de Romeo Sozzi, on peut voir un guéridon «Pigmée», avec une lampe dessinée par Christian Liaigre, comme le tabouret «Negato» en bois massif. Le sol est couvert de parquet.
Ci-dessus, à gauche: le couloir qui mène au séjour; on entrevoit au fond le tabouret de Christian Liaigre et la cheminée.
Ci-dessu, à droite: La porte au fond du couloir donne accès à la cuisine, qui reçoit la lumière grâce à la paroi à demi vitrée la séparant de la chambre à coucher.

Previous pages, left: the group of the "case a torre" (the flat is in the house in the middle).
Previous pages, right: the staircase with double-height steps in the bedroom leading to an intermediate floor over the bathroom, which is used as a storeroom. The flush-lighting units are glass fronted and were designed by Giuseppe Chigiotti.
Facing page: the living room. On the trolley designed by Alvar Aalto is a watering can from the "Milano" collection by Riccardo Dalisi.

The chairs are by Thoret. Next to the "Bergère" armchair by Romeo Sozzi there is a "Pigmée" pedestal table with a lamp by Christian Liaigre, who also designed the solid-wood "Negato" stool. The floorboards are in wood.
Above left: the corridor leading to the living room, where the Christian Liaigre stool and the fireplace can be seen in the background.
Above right: the door at the end of the corridor leading to the kitchen, which is lit by a glassed half wall that separates it from the bedroom.

Vorhergehende Doppelseite, links: der gesamte Komplex der »case a torre« (die Wohnung befindet sich im mittleren Gebäude).
Vorhergehende Doppelseite, rechts: Über die versetzten Stufen der Treppe im Schlafzimmer gelangt man auf den Hängeboden über dem Bad, der als Ankleideraum dient. Die unter einer Glasscheibe liegenden Lichtquellen entwarf Giuseppe Chigiotti.
Linke Seite: der Wohnraum mit Parkettboden. Auf dem Servierwagen von Alvar Aalto befindet sich eine Gießkanne aus Riccardo Dalisis Serie »Milano«. Die Armlehnstühle sind von Thonet. Neben dem gepolsterten Armlehnsessel »Bergère« von Romeo Sozzi steht das Tischchen »Pigmée« mit einer Leuchte von Christian Liaigre. Von ihm stammt auch der Massivholz-Hocker »Negato«.
Oben links: Der schmale Flur führt zum Wohnraum. Im Hintergrund erkennt man vor dem Kamin einen Hocker von Christian Liaigre.
Oben rechts: Durch die Tür am Ende des Flurs gelangt man in die Küche, die über die halb verglaste Trennwand zum Schlafzimmer mit Licht versorgt wird.

Le destin de cette maison, située à Orgia au sud de Sienne, semble être lié aux artistes, de Lorenzo di Pietro, dit Il Vecchietta (vers 1412–1480), à Eva-Maria Arnds von Berlepsch aujourd'hui. Petite-fille de Hans Karl Eduard von Berlepsch-Valendas (1849–1921), le pionnier de l'Art nouveau en Allemagne du Sud et en Suisse, elle sculpte et peint et ses œuvres parcourent le monde. Podere Il Leccio enchante le spectateur avec ses murs pleins d'aspérités, ses tuiles tachées de mousse, une grande cheminée, un four à pain et un jardin qui fleurit onze mois par an. Les meubles sont extrêmement simples: sièges en rotin, bancs de bois; un grand nombre d'étagères, de divisions basses, de niches pour poser livres et bibelots sont en maçonnerie. Pleine de fantaisie, Eva-Maria recycle volontiers des éléments pour créer des objets utilitaires – porte transformée en plateau de table, volets en portes d'armoire murale ...

Eva-Maria Arnds von Berlepsch

It has always been the fate of this property, situated at Orgia south of Siena, to belong to artists. In the 15th century Lorenzo di Pietro, known as il Vecchietta (c. 1412–1480), lived here; today the owner is Eva-Maria Arnds von Berlepsch, granddaughter of Hans Karl Eduard von Berlepsch-Valendas (1849–1921), forerunner of Art Nouveau in southern Germany and Switzerland. Eva-Maria herself paints and sculpts. She loves Podere Il Leccio with its rugged walls, moss-grey tiles, huge fireplace, oven for baking bread and a garden that is in flower eleven months of the year. Many of the bookshelves and partition walls are unfaced brick, as are the niches where bric-à-brac, or more books, can be tucked away. Things get recycled, such as the old door now used as a table-top or the blinds that have been turned into doors for built-in wardrobes. Eva-Maria's imagination dreams up highly practical objects that are also potent images and works of art.

Im 15. Jahrhundert lebte in diesem Haus in Orgia bei Siena der Künstler Lorenzo di Pietro, genannt il Vecchietta (um 1412–1480) – heute wohnt hier Eva-Maria Arnds von Berlepsch, die Enkelin von Hans Karl Eduard von Berlepsch-Valendas (1849–1921), dem Wegbereiter des Jugendstils in Süddeutschland und der Schweiz. Eva-Maria ist eine international bekannte Bildhauerin und Malerin, deren Werke in der ganzen Welt ausgestellt werden. Podere Il Leccio verlockt zur Muße, mit seinem rauhen Mauerwerk, den moosbewachsenen Ziegeln, dem großen Kamin und dem Ofen zum Brotbacken. Fast das ganze Jahr über blühen im Garten Blumen. Die Einrichtung ist schlicht gehalten: rustikale Möbel wie Holzbänke oder Korbstühle, Regale und Raumteiler aus einfachem Mauerwerk. Allerdings läßt sich die überbordende Phantasie von Eva-Maria Arnds von Berlepsch nicht zügeln: so werden eine alte Tür zur Tischplatte und Fensterläden zu Wandschranktüren umfunktioniert.

Page de gauche: Eva-Maria Arnds von Berlepsch; «Nature morte aux fleurs», peinture à la détrempe; «Réunis», sculpture en grès.
Ci-dessus: un coin du jardin.
A droite: Podere Il Leccio

Facing page: Eva-Maria Arnds von Berlepsch; "Still life with Flowers" in tempera; the sandstone sculpture "United".
Above: a secluded corner of the garden.
Right: Podere Il Leccio.

Linke Seite: Eva-Maria Arnds von Berlepsch; »Stilleben mit Blumen« in Tempera; die Sandsteinskulptur »Vereint«.
Oben: ein ruhiger Winkel im Garten.
Rechts: Podere Il Leccio.

Ci-dessus: *Cette pièce est divisée en deux parties distinctes par un mur percé d'un grand arc de brique; d'un côté, Eva-Maria range tout son matériel d'artiste, de l'autre, elle stocke le bois pour l'hiver.*
Page de droite: *au premier plan, un panier plein de cailloux, aux murs, des dessins et au fond, au-delà de l'arc de pierre, une sculpture de la maîtresse de maison.*

Above: *A wall with a brick arch set into it divides this room into two distinct areas; one for the artist's equipment and the other to hold firewood for the winter.*
Facing page: *a basket of stones in the foreground, and drawings lining the walls. A sculpture by Eva-Maria stands on the table on the other side of the stone arch.*

Oben: *Ein großer Rundbogen unterteilt diesen Raum. Vorne befindet sich das Arbeitsgerät der Künstlerin, hinten lagert das Brennholz für den Winter.*
Rechte Seite: *Das Obergeschoß des Hauses schmücken Zeichnungen und Skulpturen der Künstlerin. Im Vordergrund befindet sich ein mit Steinen gefüllter Korb.*

Ci-dessus: dans la cuisine, des étagères chargées d'assiettes, de
cruches et de théières.
Page de droite: un angle de la cuisine, avec la porte arquée qui
menait aux écuries.

Above: a wall unit in the kitchen with plates, jugs and teapots.
Facing page: the corner of the kitchen with the archway that used to
lead to the stables.

Oben: ein Hängeregal in der Küche mit Tellern, Krügen und Tee-
kannen.
Rechte Seite: Teilansicht der Küche. Die Rundbogentür führte früher
zu den Ställen.

Tuscany Interiors   Eva-Maria Arnds von Berlepsch

Les pérégrinations de Joyce Dittemore l'ont menée du nord de la Californie, où elle est née, à la Toscane, en passant par Paris et Bordeaux, où elle a étudié la littérature française. Il y a douze ans, elle s'est d'abord installée au Podere Maraviglia, une ferme vieille de quatre siècles au moins, dans les environs d'Arezzo. Maintenant, elle réside ailleurs; pourtant elle continue à entretenir sa ferme, où elle cultive les oliviers et la lavande et produit du miel. Les murs extérieurs sont en pierre apparente et à l'intérieur ils présentent la couleur de la terre de Toscane. La maison aux pavements de brique abrite de vieux meubles peints, des sièges rustiques en bois et d'autres en fer, réalisés par un forgeron des environs. L'ameublement a été entièrement conçu par Joyce Dittemore, qui s'occupe aujourd'hui avec succès de décoration d'intérieurs.

Joyce Dittemore

Joyce Dittemore has come a long way and done a lot of things since she left Northern California. Before moving to the countryside near Arezzo, where she now lives, she studied French literature in Paris and Bordeaux and worked in Florence. The estate of Podere Maraviglia was her first home in the area twelve years ago. She now lives elsewhere, but she has kept the estate and still comes back to look after Villa Maraviglia, where she tends her olive trees, grows lavender and makes honey. The building itself is at least 400 years old. Faced in plain stone on the outside, inside Podere Maraviglia has walls the same colour as the red soil of Tuscany. The floors are in terracotta and the painted antique furniture is flanked by wooden, country-style chairs and others made from iron by a local smith. The décor is Joyce Dittemore's own work, for today she is a successful interior designer.

Die gebürtige Kalifornierin Joyce Dittemore studierte in Paris sowie Bordeaux französische Literatur und arbeitete in Florenz, bis sie sich auf dem Land in der Nähe von Arezzo niederließ. Das war vor zwölf Jahren. Mittlerweile ist sie wieder umgezogen, aber sie hat ihr erstes Haus, Podere Maraviglia, behalten und pflanzt dort weiterhin Lavendel, erntet Oliven und stellt ihren eigenen Honig her. Das Gebäude ist mindestens vierhundert Jahre alt. Während die Außenmauern in unverputztem Stein belassen sind, leuchten die Wände im Innern in den warmen Erdtönen der Toskana. Auf dem Boden aus Terrakotta-Ziegeln stehen alte bemalte Möbel neben rustikalen Holzstühlen und Sitzgelegenheiten aus Eisen, die ein ortsansässiger Schmied hergestellt hat. Joyce Dittemore, die heute eine gefragte Innenarchitektin ist, hat schon damals die gesamte Einrichtung selbst zusammengestellt.

Page précédente: un détail évocateur du mur externe, en pierre apparente, avec une minuscule fenêtre peinte de couleur lavande.
A droite: Au-delà de la porte, surmontée d'un luminaire fait d'une tuile renversée, on entrevoit une chambre à coucher. Sur l'armoire, à droite, peinte de couleur lavande, on peut voir une curieuse lampe en forme de dragon.
Ci-dessous: le séjour, avec son divan et ses fauteuils revêtus de coton. Les lampes et la chaise en fer ont été fabriquées sur place.

Previous page: the villa's stone-faced external wall with a tiny lavender-blue window.
Right: A wall-mounted light fitting made from an upside-down roof tile shows the way through to one of the bedrooms. An unusual dragon-shaped lamp stands on top of the lavender-blue wardrobe on the right.
Below: A cotton-upholstered, three-piece suite stands in the living room. The lamps and the iron chair were made locally.

Vorhergehende Seite: ein stimmungsvolles Ensemble unter dem lavendelfarben gestrichenen Fenster. Die Mauern bestehen aus unverputztem Stein.
Rechts: Eine Lampe in Form eines umgedrehten Dachziegels beleuchtet den Eingang zu einem Schlafzimmer. Auf dem lavendelfarbenen Schrank rechts befindet sich eine originelle Leuchte in Drachenform.
Unten: Im Wohnraum steht eine mit hellem Baumwollstoff bezogene Sitzgruppe. Die Leuchten und den Eisenstuhl stellten ortsansässige Handwerker her.

Ci-dessus: *la salle à manger, avec sa cheminée. La table de bois a été trouvée dans un marché aux puces, alors que le siège en fer a été fabriqué sur place, d'après un modèle du 18e siècle. Le lustre provient d'une maison d'Arezzo. Par l'ouverture de gauche, on entrevoit le séjour; un ange en bois polychrome du 17e siècle est accroché au mur.*
A droite: *une chambre à coucher; les têtes de lit en fer forgé ont été réalisées par un forgeron des environs.*

Above: *the corner fireplace in the dining room. The wood table was picked up at a market and the iron chair was made locally to an 18th-century design. The chandelier came from a house in Arezzo. To the left is the living room, where a painted wooden angel carved in the 17th century decorates the back wall.*
Right: *one of the first-floor bedrooms. The wrought-iron heads of the two single beds were made at a local smithy.*

Oben: *das Speisezimmer mit seinem Kamin. Den Holztisch entdeckte Joyce auf einem Trödelmarkt; den Eisenstuhl hat ein ortsansässiger Schmied nach einer Zeichnung aus dem 18. Jahrhundert angefertigt. Der Leuchter stammt aus einem Haus in Arezzo. Im Wohnraum hängt eine bemalte Engelsfigur aus dem 17. Jahrhundert an der Wand.*
Rechts: *ein Schlafzimmer im ersten Geschoß. Die schmiedeeisernen Kopfteile stammen ebenfalls aus einer ortsansässigen Schmiede.*

Isanna Generali est une artiste née à Modène, en Emilie, mais elle est florentine d'adoption, car elle a enseigné de longues années la peinture décorative à l'Institut d'art de Florence. Avec son compagnon, Peter Steckenbauer, elle a cherché en vain pendant vingt ans une maison-atelier idéale, à la campagne. Et par un pur hasard, un jour qu'ils circulaient en voiture, ils se sont engagés sur une petite route perdue sans issue, près de Radi di Monteroni d'Arbia, au sud de Sienne. Elle aboutissait à une ferme abandonnée. Aujourd'hui encore, bien qu'ils y habitent depuis quatre ans, ils s'étonnent d'avoir réussi à la louer. Dans la grande maison silencieuse et dans son atelier, Isanna a trouvé l'isolement et le recueillement qu'elle cherchait et Peter la concentration dont il a besoin pour continuer à exercer son dur métier d'assistant social.

Podere San Niccolò

Isanna Generali is an artist who was born in Modena, Emilia, but whose adopted home is Florence, where she used to teach pictorial decoration at the Institute of Art. She was looking for an ideal house and studio in the country to share with her partner, Peter Steckenbauer. The search took twenty years and indeed it was only sheer chance that they happened to drive one day down a lane – apparently leading nowhere – not too far from Radi di Monteroni d'Arbia, south of Siena. At the end of the lane, they found an abandoned farmhouse. Even now, four years after moving in, they cannot believe how easy it was to secure it. Here in the silence of the big house enveloping her studio, Isanna has at last found the seclusion and meditative peace she was looking for, while Peter can recharge his batteries before going back to his demanding job as a social worker.

Durch reinen Zufall entdeckten die Künstlerin Isanna Generali und ihr Lebensgefährte Peter Steckenbauer ihr Traumhaus im wunderschönen Hügelland des Chianti. Das verlassene »podere«, ein ehemaliges Landgut, erwartete sie, als sie mit dem Auto in eine abgelegene schmale Straße bei Radi di Monteroni d'Arbia, südlich von Siena, einbogen. Zwanzig Jahre lang hatte die ehemalige Dozentin für Dekorationsmalerei am Kunstinstitut von Florenz ein geeignetes Haus gesucht – und dann passierte alles ganz von selbst. Noch heute können Isanna und Peter nicht fassen, daß sie schon vier Jahre hier wohnen. In dem großen, stillen Haus hat Isanna, die eigentlich aus Modena in der Emilia stammt, ihr Atelier eingerichtet. Hier findet sie die ersehnte Ruhe und Abgeschiedenheit, während Peter sich von seiner Tätigkeit als Sozialarbeiter erholt.

Double page précédente, à gauche: un vase avec des rameaux; le bâtiment voisin de la maison, où l'on stocke le foin au début de l'été.
Double page précédente, à droite: une sculpture d'Isanna Generali, qui fait partie de sa série des «Abiti», en grillage métallique et en plâtre.
Ci-dessus: une pièce de l'atelier aménagé dans les anciennes écuries.

Previous pages, left: a vase with twigs; the building near the house where hay is stored at the beginning of summer.
Previous pages, right: a sculpture by Isanna Generali from her series "Abiti" in wire mesh and plaster.
Above: one of the rooms in the studio that has been created in what used to be the stables.

Vorhergehende Doppelseite, links: eine Vase mit Zweigen; der Schuppen, in dem ab Anfang Sommer das Heu gelagert wird.
Vorhergehende Doppelseite, rechts: eine Skulptur von Isanna Generali aus ihrer Serie »Abiti«, Werke aus Metallnetz und Gips.
Oben: ein Atelierraum in den ehemaligen Stallungen.

Une autre partie de l'atelier avec différents outils et œuvres de l'artiste. Au mur, sous la petite fenêtre rectangulaire, est accrochée une série de cinq photos sur le personnage de la bienheureuse Ludovica Albertoni créé par le fameux sculpteur Le Bernin en 1675/76. Sur la table, les têtes de plâtre sont en cours d'élaboration. La figure de gauche fait partie d'une série d'œuvres.

Another of the rooms in the studio containing utensils and a collection of work, like the series of five photographs of the Blessed Ludovica by the famous sculptor Gian Lorenzo Bernini dating from 1675/76 under the small rectangular window. The heads on the trestle table are unfinished while the figure on the left of the photograph is part of a series of works.

Ein weiterer Atelierraum mit verschiedenen Utensilien und Werken der Künstlerin. Unter dem kleinen rechteckigen Fenster hängt eine fünfteilige Fotoserie Isannas von der Skulptur der Seligen Ludovica Albertoni, die der berühmte Bildhauer Gian Lorenzo Bernini 1675/76 schuf. Auf dem Arbeitstisch stehen einige unvollendete Gipsköpfe. Die Figur links ist Teil einer Werkserie.

Une chambre meublée, comme toute la maison, d'éléments de récupération provenant des précédentes habitations. Au mur, à droite de la fenêtre, on peut voir une œuvre d'Isanna Generali.

A bedroom furnished, like the rest of the house, with items that have come from the couple's previous homes. On the wall to the right of the window is a work by Isanna Generali.

Wie alle anderen Räume ist auch dieses Schlafzimmer mit Möbeln eingerichtet, die das Paar bereits besaß. An der Wand rechts neben dem Fenster befindet sich ein Werk von Isanna Generali.

En haut à gauche, dans le sens des aiguilles d'une montre: sur l'arête d'un mur, entre la cuisine et le séjour, une œuvre d'Isanna Generali, «Paysage siennois», composéé de petites vaches blanches; la chambre «bleu clair», avec un lit d'enfant qu'Isanna utilise pour poser les travaux de couture; un petit mouton déniché sur un marché; un chapeau et une robe de mariée trouvés sur un marché aux puces, dont Isanna s'est souvent inspirée pour ses travaux.

Clockwise from top left: on the corner of a wall between the kitchen and the living room is Isanna's work "Sienese Landscape", which incorporates a number of small white cows; the "blue" bedroom, with the cot that Isanna uses as a sewing box; a lamb that came from a market; a hat and a wedding dress, both bought at a flea market, which have often provided Isanna with inspiration.

Im Uhrzeigersinn von links oben: Isanna Generalis Werk »Landschaft bei Siena« mit kleinen weißen Kühen befindet sich auf der Wandkante zwischen Küche und Wohnraum; das sogenannte »blaue« Schlafzimmer mit einem Kinderbett, in dem Isanna ihre Näharbeiten aufbewahrt; ein Schäfchen, das die Künstlerin auf einem kleinen Markt entdeckte; ein Hut und ein Brautkleid, das sie auf einem Flohmarkt erstanden und das Isanna oft als Inspirationsquelle für ihre Arbeit gedient hat.

Montalcino e la Maremma

Juché sur une colline de Montalcino, le Château du Romitorio, construit au 13e siècle, a jadis fait office de prison et de couvent. Sandro Chia, peintre et sculpteur italien, l'a acheté en 1986. Il se trouvait alors dans un état pitoyable. Non content de le restaurer, il a également planté des oliviers, des arbres fruitiers et des hectares de vignobles, qui donnent aujourd'hui un excellent brunello. L'ameublement du château est très éclectique: des meubles Biedermeier jouxtent des fauteuils du 18e siècle, des tables art déco, des amphores étrusques et des sarcophages égyptiens. En outre, Sandro Chia a disséminé çà et là, dans les recoins les plus inattendus du château, de petites figures dessinées au crayon sur les murs.

Sandro Chia

In 1986, the painter and sculptor Sandro Chia bought the castle known as "Il Romitorio", or the hermitage, which stands on a hill near Montalcino. At the time, it was in a distressingly poor state of repair. Chia not only renovated the fabric of the building, which dates from the 13th century and has been used both as a prison and a monastery, he also changed the landscape around it by planting olive groves, orchards and, most importantly, several hectares of vineyards. Today these produce one of the finest Brunellos you could hope to find in your glass. Inside, Il Romitorio is an attractive hotchpotch of styles. Biedermeier furniture and 18th-century armchairs jostle with Art Nouveau tables and archaeological remains, including Etruscan amphorae and Egyptian sarcophagi. On the walls next to the telephone and in other odd corners, are small figures drawn by Chia in pencil.

Der italienische Maler und Bildhauer Sandro Chia gehört heute zu den Spitzenerzeugern von Brunello di Montalcino, einem der bekanntesten Rotweine Italiens. Bemerkenswert ist auch das Domizil des Künstlers, das Castello Il Romitorio, das er 1986 in einem erbärmlichen Zustand kaufte. Chia restaurierte die Burg aus dem 13. Jahrhundert, die im Lauf ihrer wechselvollen Geschichte schon als Gefängnis und als Kloster diente. Auch die Umgebung gestaltete er nach seinen Wünschen, pflanzte Oliven- und Obstbäume, vor allem aber mehrere Hektar Wein an. Mittlerweile hat der Künstler in den alten Räumen ein originelles Ambiente geschaffen, in dem verschiedene Stilrichtungen frech und unbekümmert nebeneinander existieren. Schlichte Biedermeiermöbel vertragen sich bestens mit üppigen Fauteuils des 18. Jahrhunderts; neben Jugendstiltischen haben etruskische Amphoren und ägyptische Sarkophage ihren Platz gefunden. Hier und da, neben dem Telefon und in versteckten Winkeln des »castello«, hat Sandro Chia mit Bleistift kleine Figuren an die Wand gezeichnet.

Tuscany Interiors   Sandro Chia

Double page précédente, à gauche: Sandro Chia avec son épouse Marella Caracciolo et leur fils; une jarre jouxte une sculpture.
Double page précédente, à droite: l'atelier aménagé sous le toit. Sandro a déniché le divan, le guéridon et les bibliothèques chez un brocanteur de Montalcino. Au mur, un grand format au fusain de Sandro. Il a peint en bleu la sculpture en plâtre du 17e siècle.
Page de gauche: dans le hall, l'abreuvoir en pierre d'époque romaine. Entre des armoiries en fer forgé, on aperçoit le dessin de Sandro pour l'étiquette de son premier vin, «Romito del Romitorio». Au-dessous, le remarquable arc en marbre, qhe Chia a maçonné dans le mur pour produire un effet dépaysant.
Ci-dessus, à gauche: Sandro Chia a gratté sa grande peinture murale pour laisser apparaître l'enduit et la pierre qui lui servent de support. Le divan anglais provient également d'un brocanteur.
Ci-dessus, à droite: La petite salle du billard renferme des œuvres de Sandro Chia et un double portrait de l'aîné de ses enfants, réinterprété par Andy Warhol.

Previous pages, left: Sandro Chia, his wife Marella Caracciolo, and their son; an ancient jar next to a statue.
Previous pages, right: Leaning against the wall in the attic studio is an untitled charcoal drawing by Sandro Chia. He discovered the sofa, the unusual table and the two bookcases in a second-hand dealer's shop in Montalcino. The statuette is a 17th-century work in plaster painted blue by Sandro Chia.
Facing page: the entry showing the Roman drinking trough. Between the two wrought-iron crests on the wall is a design by Sandro Chia for the label of the first wine produced on the castle estate, "Romito del Romitorio". The arch beyond is a piece of marble Chia found and incorporated into the wall to produce a disorienting visual effect.

Above left: a large mural in the dining room by Sandro Chia, which has been scraped away to reveal the plaster and stone underneath. The sofa is English and came from a second-hand dealer.
Above right: A number of works by Sandro Chia are on display in the small billiard room together with a double portrait of his eldest child, reworked by Andy Warhol.

Vorhergehende Doppelseite, links: Sandro Chia mit seiner Ehefrau Marella Caracciolo und ihrem Sohn; ein Ölkrug neben einer Skulptur.
Vorhergehende Doppelseite, rechts: das Atelier im Dachgeschoß. Das Sofa, den ungewöhnlichen Tisch und die beiden Bücherschränke hat Chia bei einem Antiquitätenhändler in Montalcino aufgestöbert. An der Wand lehnt eine großformatige Kohlezeichnung des Künstlers. Die Gipsskulptur aus dem 17. Jahrhundert hat er blau bemalt.
Linke Seite: die Steintränke aus römischer Zeit im Eingangsbereich. Zwischen den schmiedeeisernen Wappen hängt Chias Entwurf für das Etikett des ersten eigenen Weins, »Romito del Romitorio«. Auffallend ist der Marmorbogen darunter, den er als Überraschungsmoment in die Wand einmauerte.
Oben links: Im Speisezimmer befindet sich über dem englischen Sofa, das ebenfalls von einem Antiquitätenhändler stammt, ein großes Wandbild Chias. Es wurde an einigen Stellen abgekratzt, bis der Putz und der darunterliegende Stein zum Vorschein kamen.
Oben rechts: das Billardzimmer mit Werken von Chia und einem Doppelporträt seines ältesten Sohns, das Andy Warhol überarbeitete.

La cheminée de la salle à manger constitue l'unique ajout architectural au château, dont la structure est restée intacte. Les chaises à l'anglaise ont été réalisées par une manufacture indienne, les pieds de table proviennent d'un monastère du 17e siècle. A droite, le tableau «Andromède et Thésée», du peintre vénitien Jacopo Palma il Giovane (1544–1628).

The chimney for the dining room fireplace is the only architectural addition to the castle, whose original structure has been left intact. The table legs came from a 17th-century friary. The English-style chairs were made in India. To the right of the dresser at the far end of the room is a painting of "Andromeda and Theseus" by Jacopo Palma il Giovane (1544–1628).

Der Kamin des Eßzimmers ist die einzige architektonische Veränderung, die Chia an dem »castello« vorgenommen hat. Die englischen Stühle fertigte eine indische Manufaktur, während das Tischgestell aus dem 17. Jahrhundert aus einem Kloster stammt. Rechts hängt das Gemälde »Andromeda und Theseus« des venezianischen Malers Jacopo Palma il Giovane (1544–1628).

Tuscany Interiors   Sandro Chia

A droite: Devant une gravure représentant le Colisée romain, divers objets, entre autres une bouteille du vin de Il Romitorio, forment une nature morte.
Ci-dessous: la cuisine avec la cheminée d'origine, ornée d'une gravure de Chia. L'armoire à appliques est un meuble typique de la région.

Right: a still-life miscellany including a bottle of wine produced at Il Romitorio. The antique print depicts the Colosseum in Rome.
Below: the kitchen. The original fireplace is adorned with an engraving by Sandro Chia. The cabinet standing against the wall on the right of the photograph is typical of the area. It was purchased from a second-hand dealer.

Rechts: Vor einem Druck mit dem Kolosseum in Rom gruppiert sich ein Stilleben aus unterschiedlichen Objekten, darunter eine auf Il Romitorio abgefüllte Weinflasche.
Unten: die Küche mit dem originalen Kamin, auf dessen Sims ein Stich von Chia lehnt. Typisch für die Region ist der Vitrinenschrank.

Ci-dessus, à gauche: la vitrine dans laquelle Sandro Chia conserve ce
qu'il appelle le «trésor des pirates».
Ci-dessus, à droite: des objets et une photo des maîtres de maison.
Page de droite: une chambre à coucher avec son plafond aux poutres
d'origine. Sandro a trouvé le lit art nouveau en fer chez un brocanteur
de Pietrasanta. Au mur, des gravures de Sandro Chia.

Above left: the display cabinet where Sandro Chia keeps what he
calls his "pirates' treasure".
Above right: the photograph shows the owners of the house.
Facing page: one of the bedrooms, showing the original beams that
support the roofing. The iron bedstead is an Art Nouveau piece that
came from a second-hand dealer in Pietrasanta. The engravings on
the walls are by Sandro Chia.

Oben links: die Vitrine, in der Sandro seinen »Piratenschatz« aufbe-
wahrt.
Oben rechts: Die Fotografie zeigt die Hausbesitzer.
Rechte Seite: In diesem Schlafzimmer befinden sich noch die Ori-
ginalholzbalken. Das eiserne Jugendstilbett hat Sandro bei einem
Antiquitätenhändler in Pietrasanta gefunden. An der Wand hängen
Stiche von Sandro Chia.

Les plus anciennes maisons de Bagno Vignoni près de San Quirico d'Orcia entourent un beau bassin alimenté par la source thermale qui jaillit au cœur du village. Le plus célèbre des Médicis, le mécène Laurent le Magnifique, venait déjà en cure dans ce village. La tradition attribue l'une des maisons à la famille de la célèbre mystique sainte Catherine de Sienne (1347–1380). Transformée autrefois en relais de poste, la maison sert de résidence secondaire à une famille romaine. Une toute nouvelle atmosphère emplit les pièces du bâtiment qui offrent plusieurs beaux points de vue sur le bassin. Elles constituent à présent l'espace parfait pour accueillir une collection d'art moderne. Un beau jardin entoure la demeure sur trois côtés. Les paysagistes, Anna Maria Scaravella et Isabella Castelli, ont conservé les espèces végétales caractéristiques de la campagne toscane et créé un jardin de plantes aromatiques.

Bagno Vignoni

The oldest houses in Bagno Vignoni, a village near San Quirico d'Orcia, cluster round a pool of thermal spring water in the centre of the village. The most famous of the Medici, art patron Lorenzo the Magnificent, took a cure here. One of the houses is said to have once belonged to the family of Saint Catherine of Siena (1347–1380), a famous mystic. Later on it became a posthouse, and today it has been converted into a second home for a family from Rome. The property offers many charming glimpses of the thermal pool. The garden, landscaped by Anna Maria Scaravella and Isabella Castelli, features trees and flowers typical of the Tuscan countryside, together with a herb garden. A new, fresh spirit now pervades the generous if austere interiors, which have become the unusual yet perfect setting for a modern art collection.

In den warmen Quellen von Bagno Vignoni, einem Dorf bei San Quirico d'Orcia, badete schon der berühmteste Medici, der große Kunstmäzen Lorenzo der Prächtige. Direkt an dem steinernen Thermalbecken im Herzen des mittelalterlichen Dorfes liegt das Haus, das einst der Familie der Heiligen Katharina von Siena (1347–1380) gehörte. Später diente es als Poststation. Heute ist es der Zweitwohnsitz einer römischen Familie, die von dem wunderschönen, auf drei Ebenen angelegten Garten aus die faszinierenden Ausblicke auf das jahrhundertealte Steinbecken genießt. Die Landschaftsgärtnerinnen Anna Maria Scaravella und Isabella Castelli beließen die typische Vegetation der Toskana und pflanzten aromatische Kräuter an. In den strengen, großzügigen Innenräumen des Gebäudes ist neuer, frischer Geist eingezogen – sie sind ungewöhnlicher und doch perfekter Rahmen für eine qualitätvolle Sammlung Moderner Kunst.

Premières pages, à gauche: *Du jardin situé à l'arrière de la maison, on découvre le bassin sur la place; dans la salle du billard, entre les deux fenêtres en plein cintre aux arcs de briques apparentes, une sculpture en plâtre de Nunzio.*

Premières pages, à droite: *détail d'une pièce du rez-de-chaussée, à côté du couloir qui dessert les chambres. On remarque deux petits fauteuils de Frank Lloyd Wright, surmontés par un grand tableau de Cy Twombly.*

Double page précédente: *vue de la maison qui domine le bassin au centre du village de Bagno Vignoni.*

Ci-dessus: *La salle du billard, au rez-de-chaussée, abrite de nombreuses œuvres d'art: un tableau du 18e siècle cohabite avec une sculpture de Lucio Fontana.*

First pages, left: *the garden behind the house, looking over the pool in the square; an eye-catching plaster sculpture by Nunzio has pride of place between two brick-framed, round-arch windows in the billiard room.*

First pages, right: *detail of one of the rooms on the ground floor. It is next to the corridor that leads to the other rooms and is furnished with two chairs by Frank Lloyd Wright under a large painting by Cy Twombly.*

Previous pages: *a view of the house that overlooks the pool in the centre of Bagno Vignoni.*

Above: *The art of the past rubs shoulders with that of the present around the 19th-century billiard table: an 18th-century painting hangs near a sculpture by Lucio Fontana.*

Eingangsseiten, links: *der Garten hinter dem Haus mit Blick auf das Thermalbad; im Billardzimmer befindet sich zwischen zwei Rundbogenfenstern mit Ziegeleinfassung eine Gipsskulptur von Nunzio.*
Eingangsseiten, rechts: *Teilansicht eines Raumes im Erdgeschoß mit Blick in den Korridor. Über zwei Sesseln von Frank Lloyd Wright hängt ein Gemälde von Cy Twombly.*
Vorhergehende Doppelseite: *Ansicht des Hauses am Thermalbecken.*
Linke Seite: *Um den Billardtisch aus dem 19. Jahrhundert sind Werke Alter Meister und moderner Künstler versammelt: ein Gemälde aus dem 18. Jahrhundert hinter einer Skulptur von Lucio Fontana.*

Ci-dessus: *La cuisine est une vaste pièce d'aspect accueillant. A côté de la cheminée, les deux vieux fauteuils en bois fabriqués dans la région sont rustiques, comme les chaises qui entourent la table de bois couverte d'un tissu de cachemire. Au mur, on peut voir une vieille affiche publicitaire.*

Above: *The generously proportioned kitchen was designed with entertaining in mind. There are two antique, locally made wooden armchairs next to the fireplace, echoing the rustic style of the wooden kitchen table covered with a paisley cloth.*

Oben: *die geräumige Küche. Die Holzstühle neben dem Kamin wurden in der Region gefertigt, ebenso wie die Stühle um den mit einem Kaschmirstoff bedeckten Tisch.*

Le propriétaire actuel, tombé amoureux du merveilleux jardin, a acheté cette résidence, située à Cetona, au sud de Montepulciano, sans même visiter l'intérieur de la maison. Cet associé d'un grand couturier n'a pas regretté son acquisition car l'architecte-décorateur Renzo Mongiardino a fait de la Villa La Vagnola, qui résulte de la réunion, au 18e siècle, de deux édifices adjacents, un véritable joyau. Aujourd'hui, certaines salles sont tapissées de papier peint imprimé à la main et abritent des céramiques inspirées des décorations du Palazzo Pitti à Florence. La décoration intérieure de la maison doit beaucoup à une série d'aquarelles datant du début du 19e siècle, acquises plus tard par le propriétaire, et représentant des intérieurs autrichiens et allemands. Mongiardino a su décorer les vastes espaces avec infiniment de discernement et de goût, et les a mis en valeur jusque dans le moindre détail.

Villa La Vagnola

Villa La Vagnola at Cetona, south of Montepulciano, took on its present form during the 18th century, when two adjacent buildings were joined to make a single structure with a marvellous garden. The present owner, partner of a world-famous couturier, will tell you that he bought the villa sight unseen, because he had actually fallen in love with the garden. The interior of the house was the work of Renzo Mongiardino and features splendid hand-printed paper and ceramics inspired by the decorations in Palazzo Pitti in Florence. A second source of inspiration was a series of early 19th-century watercolours of Austrian and German interiors. Currently on display in the winter garden, they bear testimony to the stylistic pedigree of the most important rooms of Villa La Vagnola.

Der heutige Besitzer kaufte La Vagnola, ohne die Innenräume zu kennen, denn er hatte sich eigentlich in den wunderschönen Garten verliebt. Dieser entstand im 18. Jahrhundert, als zwei benachbarte Häuser zu einer Villa zusammengefaßt wurden. Den Kauf hat der Partner eines berühmten Modeschöpfers nicht bereut, denn der Innenarchitekt Renzo Mongiardino hat die Villa in Cetona, südlich von Montepulciano, zu einem echten Juwel umgestaltet. Einige Räume wurden nach dem Vorbild des Florentiner Palazzo Pitti mit handbedruckten Tapeten dekoriert und mit erlesenem Porzellan ausgestattet. Später erwarb der Besitzer eine wertvolle Aquarellserie mit österreichischen und deutschen Interieurs aus dem frühen 19. Jahrhundert, die Mongiardino eine Fülle von Inspirationen lieferte und heute im Wintergarten ausgestellt ist. Mit viel Fingerspitzengefühl hat er die großzügigen Räumlichkeiten geschmackvoll und bis ins letzte Detail durchdacht eingerichtet.

Double page précédente, à droite: *la pièce qui donne accès à la salle à manger, avec ses meubles italiens du 19e siècle. Le pavement est en marbre et en céramique locale, alors que la décoration murale s'inspire du Palazzo Pitti de Florence.*
Ci-dessus: *le jardin de la Villa La Vagnola, réaménagé par l'architecte paysagiste Paolo Peyrone. Au fond, le bâtiment des écuries, transformé en orangerie, abrite un gymnase au premier étage.*

Previous pages, right: *The connecting room leading from the dining room is furnished with 19th-century Italian furniture. The floor is in marble and local terracotta, while the décor was inspired by Palazzo Pitti in Florence.*
Above: *the garden of Villa La Vagnola, redesigned by the landscape architect Paolo Peyrone. In the background is the former stable building, now an orangery with a gymnasium on the first floor.*

Vorhergehende Doppelseite, rechts: *der Durchgangssaal zum Speisezimmer mit italienischen Möbeln aus dem 19. Jahrhundert. Der Fußboden besteht aus Marmor und lokalem Terrakotta. Vorbild für die weitere Ausstattung ist der Florentiner Palazzo Pitti.*
Oben: *Der Garten der Villa wurde von dem Landschaftsarchitekten Paolo Peyrone neu strukturiert. Im Hintergrund sieht man das Gebäude, in dem früher die Stallungen untergebracht waren. Heute überwintern dort die Pflanzen, und im ersten Stock hat sich der Hausherr einen Fitneßraum eingerichtet.*

A droite: vue d'une partie du jardin. Les obélisques correspondent au
goût du 18e siècle.
Ci-dessous: Le jardin d'hiver abrite un mobilier anglais du 19e siècle.

Right: a view of the garden. The obelisk was a fashionable motif in
the 18th century.
Below: The winter garden features 19th-century English furniture.

Rechts: Teilansicht des Gartens. Die Obelisken entsprechen dem Geschmack des 18. Jahrhunderts.
Unten: Der Wintergarten ist mit englischen Möbelstücken aus dem
19. Jahrhundert eingerichtet.

Ci-dessus: le séjour principal. Les colonnes en trompe-l'œil, multi-pliant celles qui sont vraiment présentes dans la pièce, ont été peintes sur le papier peint mural du 19e siècle imitant des tentures. Sur la table, on peut voir des cristaux anciens de Baccarat.
Page de droite: un détail du séjour. Le divan Empire, sur lequel est installée Olivia, un king-charles, appartenait à la princesse Mathilde, nièce de Napoléon. Le tableau, un double portrait féminin, date du 19e siècle.

Above: the main living room. The "trompe-l'œil" columns, replacing ones that actually adorned the room, were painted onto 19th-century wallpaper with a pattern of imitation drapes. The glassware on the table is antique Baccarat.
Facing page: detail of the living room. The Empire-style settee on which Olivia, a King Charles spaniel, is relaxing once belonged to Napoleon's niece, Princess Mathilde. The painting with the double female portrait dates from the 19th century.

Oben: der Hauptwohnraum. Auf eine Tapete mit »Trompe-l'œil«-Vorhängen aus dem 19. Jahrhundert wurden Säulen aufgemalt, die den echten im Raum gleichen. Auf dem Tisch steht altes Baccarat-Kristall.
Rechte Seite: Ansicht des Wohnraums. Das Empire-Sofa, auf dem sich King Charles Spaniel Olivia ausruht, gehörte einst Prinzessin Mathilde, einer Nichte Napoleons. Das Doppelporträt stammt aus dem 19. Jahrhundert.

Dans le séjour, des deux côtés de la cheminée sur laquelle est installée
une petite collection de vases italiens du 19e siècle, on peut noter deux
tableaux de l'école de Francisco de Zurbarán.

To the sides of the living room fireplace, on which is displayed a small
collection of 19th-century Italian vases, there are two impressive
paintings from the School of Francisco de Zurbarán.

Auf dem Kaminsims im Wohnraum befindet sich eine kleine Sammlung italienischer Vasen aus dem 19. Jahrhundert. Links und rechts
vom Kamin hängen Gemälde aus der Schule von Francisco de Zurbarán.

A droite: Le jardin d'hiver aux parois vitrées, conçu par Renzo Mongiardino pour offrir une transition entre la villa et le jardin, abrite un mobilier anglais du 19e siècle. Au premier plan, on note des statuettes chinoises et deux vases de Meissen.

Ci-dessous: Le dressing-room a été entièrement conçu par Renzo Mongiardino, à l'exception de la banquette-lit suédoise du 19e siècle.

Double page suivante: les aquarelles du 19e siècle représentent des intérieurs autrichiens et allemands qui ont inspiré Renzo Mongiardino pour décorer la Villa La Vagnola. Les objets de verre colorés sont d'origine italienne et allemande.

Right: The glassed-walled winter garden created by Renzo Mongiardino to link the villa to its garden features 19th-century English furniture. Chinese statuettes and two Meissen vases can be seen in the foreground.

Below: The dressing room was designed throughout by Renzo Mongiardino, with the exception of the 19th-century Swedish day-bed.

Following pages: the watercolours of 19th-century Austrian and German interiors that inspired Renzo Mongiardino's décor at Villa La Vagnola. The coloured glassware is of Italian and German manufacture.

Rechts: Der Wintergarten mit englischen Möbeln aus dem 19. Jahrhundert verbindet Villa und Garten miteinander. Im Vordergrund sind chinesische Statuetten und zwei Vasen aus Meißener Porzellan zu sehen.

Unten: Die Ausstattung des Ankleidezimmers entwarf Renzo Mongiardino. Lediglich die schwedische Bettcouch stammt aus dem 19. Jahrhundert.

Folgende Doppelseite: Die Aquarelle – österreichische und deutsche Interieurs aus dem 19. Jahrhundert – inspirierten Renzo Mongiardino bei der Innenausstattung der Villa La Vagnola. Die Gefäße aus farbigem Glas sind italienischer und deutscher Herkunft.

Le séjour entièrement conçu sur maquette par Renzo Mongiardino,
a été reconstitué sur place dans le moindre détail. Les fauteuils sont
recouverts d'un tissu moderne brodé au petit point.

The entire design of the living room was drafted in Renzo Mongiardino's studio before being painstakingly recreated on-site. The
chairs are upholstered in a delicately stitched modern fabric.

Renzo Mongiardino erstellte in seinem Atelier ein Modell des gesamten Wohnraums, das dann bis ins kleinste Detail verwirklicht wurde.
Die Sitzmöbel sind mit einem modernen Petit-Point-Stoff bezogen.

Tuscany Interiors   Villa La Vagnola

La salle de lecture jouxte la bibliothèque, où les livres sont rangés dans des armoires vitrées inspirées d'un ancien dessin vénitien. La fonction du beau poêle de céramique vert et blanc de la fin du 18e siècle, à côté de la duchesse Louis XV, est uniquement décorative.

The study leads through to the library, where the books are stored in a bookcase inspired by a old Venetian design. The impressive late 18th-century green and white ceramic stove standing next to the Louis Quinze duchesse seat is used for decoration only.

Das Lesezimmer. Der üppig verzierte Ofen aus grüner und weißer Keramik aus dem späten 18. Jahrhundert hat lediglich dekorative Funktion. Daneben ein mit Duchesse bezogenes Louis-Quinze-Sofa. Im Hintergrund schließt sich die Bibliothek an, deren Bücherschränke nach einer alten venezianischen Zeichnung entstanden sind.

Page de gauche: *La chambre du maître de maison a conservé son plafond d'origine. Le lit en gondole à baldaquin et le tapis au petit point datent du 19e siècle.*
Ci-dessus: *Une série en sceaux en plâtre victoriens décore une partie de la chambre à coucher du maître de maison.*

Facing page: *In the master bedroom, the original ceiling has been preserved. The four-poster bed and finely woven carpet date from the 19th century.*
Above: *A collection of Victorian plaster seals adorns one of the walls in the main bedroom.*

Linke Seite: *Das Schlafzimmer des Hausherrn schmückt die original erhaltene Deckenbemalung. Das Himmelbett und der Petit-Point-Teppich stammen aus dem 19. Jahrhundert.*
Oben: *eine Sammlung von viktorianischen Gipssiegeln im Schlafzimmer des Hausherrn.*

Datant du 15e siècle, cette ferme de San Casciano dei Bagni est à la fois une maison de vacances et le siège d'une association culturelle réputée, «Chartarius», qui organise des cours de restauration d'œuvres anciennes sur papier et de photographies anciennes. L'architecte Giacomo Bianchi l'a restructurée et a aménagé les salles de cours et le laboratoire dans les deux bâtiments agricoles unis au corps principal de la maison. Dans la mesure du possible, il a cherché à préserver l'esprit de l'édifice où habitaient plusieurs familles paysannes. La partie destinée à l'habitation, répartie sur deux étages, est aménagée de façon simple et fonctionnelle; elle ne comporte que les rares meubles indispensables, pour mettre en valeur les structures, le rythme aéré des grandes pièces et le charme des matériaux traditionnels: la brique des pavements, les poutres apparentes, le fer forgé.

Podere Ráncioli

Podere Ráncioli at San Casciano dei Bagni is a 15th-century farmhouse, which was built to accommodate several families of farmworkers. Today it serves both as a holiday residence and as the headquarters of "Chartarius", an important arts organization which runs courses in the restoration of historic works on paper and old photographs. The restoration of Podere Ráncioli was supervised by the architect Giacomo Bianchi, who converted the two farm buildings that adjoin the main living area of the house into classrooms and a workshop. Furniture of the living area has been kept to a bare minimum so as not to detract from the imposing structural features, the generous dimensions of the light-filled rooms, the interesting terracotta floor and the beamed ceilings, which are complemented in the traditional manner by wrought-iron or painted surfaces.

Das bekannte Kunstinstitut »Chartarius« bietet Lehrgänge für die Restaurierung von Zeichnungen, Radierungen und anderen Papierarbeiten sowie von historischen Fotografien an. Unterrichtsräume und Werkstatt befinden sich in den beiden Nebenflügeln des Podere Ráncioli in San Casciano dei Bagni, das aus dem 15. Jahrhundert stammt. Ursprünglich wohnten in dem zweistöckigen »podere« mehrere Bauernfamilien. Heute wird es auch als Ferienhaus genutzt. Den Umbau nahm der Architekt Giacomo Bianchi vor, der die wunderschönen originalen Terrakotta-Fußböden und die alten hölzernen Deckenbalken bewahrte. Die großzügigen Räume wurden mit einigen wenigen, notwendigen Möbelstücken einfach und praktisch eingerichtet. Auffallend schön sind die ortstypischen schmiedeeisernen und lackierten Arbeiten.

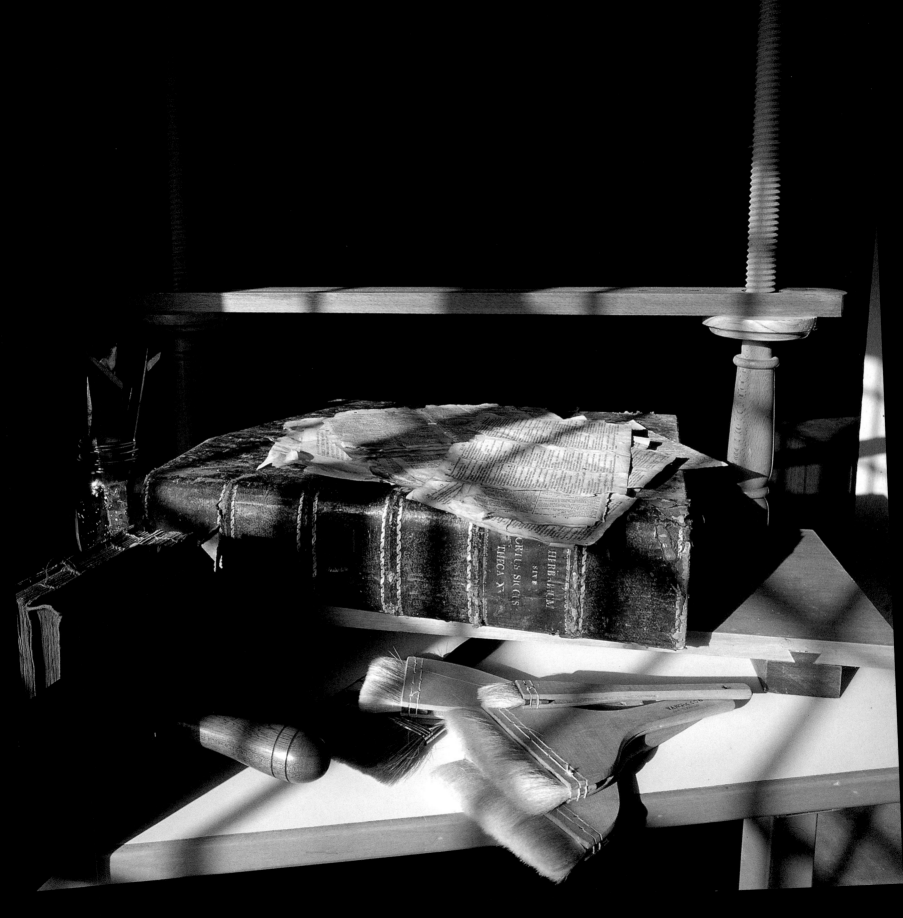

Double page précédente, à droite: *A l'aide de différents outils et matériaux, les œuvres d'art et les photographies historiques sont restaurées dans le laboratoire.*
Ci-dessus: *vue partielle du laboratoire. Les deux boîtes à lumière sont utilisées pour restaurer des photographies. On aperçoit divers outils, entre autres une presse de compression à papier. On reconnaît la bergerie d'origine aux matériaux typiques que sont la terre cuite, le bois et le fer, et que l'on retrouve dans tout le «podere». Toutes les lampes sont de fabrication industrielle.*

Previous pages, right: *Works of art and historic photographs are restored in the laboratory using various instruments and materials.*
Above: *part of the laboratory. The two illuminated slide-viewing boxes are used in the restoration of photographs. The laboratory equipment includs a paper-printing press. Converted from a sheep fold, the space*

features the characteristic terracotta, wood and iron found throughout the "podere". All the lighting is of industrial design.

Vorhergehende Doppelseite, rechts: *Mit verschiedenen Werkzeugen und Materialien werden im Labor Kunstwerke und historische Fotografien restauriert.*
Oben: *Teilansicht des Labors. Die beiden Leuchtkästen werden bei der Restaurierung von Fotos eingesetzt. Hier gibt es verschiedene Werkzeuge, unter anderem eine Papierdruckpresse. Den ursprünglichen Schafstall charakterisieren die typischen Materialien Terrakotta, Holz und Eisen, die sich im gesamten »podere« wiederfinden. Alle Leuchten stammen aus industrieller Produktion.*

La salle à manger avec sa table de la fin du 19e siècle et des chaises rustiques fabriquées dans la région. Les carrelages en brique d'origine et les vieilles poutres en bois ont été conservés. Au-dessus de la table est suspendue une lampe dans un abat-jour tout simple. La persienne de la petite fenêtre à double croisée protège des froidures de l'hiver et des températures estivales.

The dining-room, featuring a fine, late 19th-century table and rustic, locally-made chairs. In this room too, the original terracotta floors and the old beamed ceiling have been preserved. Above the table hangs a lamp with a simple shade. The "persiana", the shutter on the small double-transom window, offers protection against the cold winter air and summer heat alike.

Das Eßzimmer mit einem Tisch vom Ende des 19. Jahrhunderts und rustikalen, in der Gegend gefertigten Stühlen. Auch in diesem Raum sind der originale Terrakotta-Fußboden und die alten hölzernen Deckenbalken erhalten geblieben. Über dem Tisch hängt eine Lampe mit einfachem Schirm. Die »persiana«, der Fensterladen des kleinen Doppelkreuzfensters, schützt vor kalter Winterluft und Sommerhitze.

La cuisine est une vaste pièce très fonctionnelle. Son pourtour est doté d'un seul et unique plan de maçonnerie revêtu de carrelage blanc, dans lequel sont insérés deux plaques de cuisson surmontées d'une grande hotte et un évier à deux bacs. En dessous, des portes au châssis de fer, en grillage métallique, ferment les placards. Au premier plan, la table se compose d'un piètement de fer et d'un plan de marbre.

The kitchen area is extensive. The layout features a continuous white-tiled brick working surface with two hobs installed under the same giant extractor hood and a double sink. The cabinets under the worktop have wire doors mounted on iron frames. The top of the table in the foreground is a marble slab that rests on an iron supporting structure.

Die durchgehende, gemauerte Arbeitsfläche in der großzügigen Küche ist mit weißen Kacheln verkleidet und verfügt über zwei Kochgelegenheiten sowie zwei Spülbecken. Die kleinen Schränke unter der Arbeitsplatte besitzen Türen aus Metallgittern mit Eisenrahmen. Im Vordergrund ist ein Eisentisch mit Marmorplatte zu sehen.

Ci-dessus: *Cette chambre au plafond à poutres apparentes et au pavement de brique d'origine est extrêmement simple; le tissu du couvre-lit est le même que celui des rideaux.*
A droite: *Dans la salle de bains, le coin douche est revêtu de terre cuite à l'ancienne, pour offrir une continuité avec le reste de la maison au niveau des matériaux.*

Above: *one of the bedrooms, with a beamed ceiling and the original terracotta floor. The bed is simply yet effectively covered in the same fabric as the curtain.*
Right: *the bathroom shower is tiled in an antique-style terracotta that blends in with the materials used elsewhere in the house.*

Oben: *ein schlichtes Schlafzimmer mit dem originalen Terrakotta-Fußboden und den noch ursprünglichen Deckenbalken aus Holz. Die Tagesdecke auf dem einfachen Bett ist aus dem gleichen Stoff wie die Vorhänge.*
Rechts: *das Badezimmer. Für einen harmonischen Gesamteindruck wurden die Terrakotta-Fliesen der Dusche den original erhaltenen Fliesen in den übrigen Räumen nachempfunden.*

Le Fontanelle – une ancienne «fattoria» – offre un agréable lieu de retraite à l'architecte et décorateur milanais Piero Castellini. «C'est la nature, affirme-t-il, qui a constitué le point de départ de mon travail de restauration». Fidèle à l'esprit des lieux, il a dégagé les belles voûtes des plafonds et choisi pour les espaces intérieurs des coloris en harmonie avec ceux de la terre de Toscane. Un de ses amis peintres, Adam Alvarez lui a procuré des pigments naturels pour les murs: les jaunes intenses et les ocres rouges évoquant ceux des paysages toscans et le mauve des couchers de soleil. Le résultat est une maison de campagne sophistiquée, à l'ameublement particulièrement éclectique, qui trahit bien l'engouement de Piero Castellini pour les tissus – il est l'héritier d'une maison productrice de toiles de lin et possède, avec son frère Emanuele, une boutique à Milan.

Piero Castellini

Fattoria Le Fontanelle is the pied-à-terre of the Milanese architect and interior designer Piero Castellini. "Nature," he tells us, "was my starting-point in planning restoration work." Remaining faithful to the spirit of the local countryside, Castellini first restored the lovely vaulted ceilings and then selected the colours for the interiors using the Tuscan landscape as his palette. Adam Alvarez, a painter and friend of Castellini's, used natural pigments on the walls in the intense yellows and ochre reds that can be seen in local fields, as well as the pale purple hues of the setting sun. Together with the highly eclectic furnishings, these tones convey the flavour of a sophisticated country residence. Piero Castellini's passion for fabrics is also quite evident, for he inherited a linen mill and runs a showroom in Milan together with his brother Emanuele.

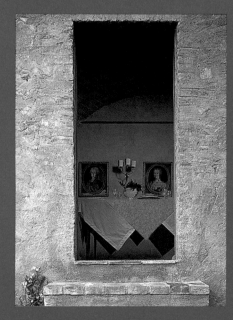

Le Fontanelle, eine ehemalige »fattoria«, ist heute das Refugium des Mailänder Architekten und Innenausstatters Piero Castellini. »Die Natur war mein Vorbild bei der Restaurierung«, erklärt er. Zunächst legte er die beeindruckenden Deckengewölbe frei und gestaltete dann die Innenräume neu. Für die Wände wählte sein Malerfreund Adam Alvarez Pigmente in den Farben der Natur: die intensiven Gelbnuancen und das rötliche Ocker der toskanischen Erde sowie das weiche Violett der Sonnenuntergänge. Als Erbe einer Leinenfabrik und Mitbesitzer eines »Show rooms« in Mailand spielen Stoffe für Piero Castellini natürlich eine große Rolle. Im Zusammenspiel mit der abwechslungsreichen Einrichtung entstand so ein perfekt durchdachtes ländliches Ambiente.

Tuscany Interiors   Piero Castellini

Premières pages, à gauche: *Fattoria Le Fontanelle; à travers la porte ouverte, on aperçoit une table et deux nappes de Castellini.*
Premières pages, à droite: *sur la cheminée, une petite collection de récipients, flacons et bougeoirs de porcelaine dans des tons bleus. Les portraits-reliefs ovales sont un travail piémontais du 18e siècle.*
Double page précédente: *Le plafond voûté du séjour de la villa est d'origine. Les sièges sont revêtus de tissus de provenances diverses, dont beaucoup ont cependant été créés par la Milanaise Mimma Gini, architecte d'intérieur; les nattes qui couvrent le sol sont de Piero Castellini lui-même. On notera la liberté d'esprit qui a présidé au choix du mobilier, unifié par des tons coordonnés.*
Page de gauche: *Cette magnifique armoire inspirée du style chinois renferme une collection de livres et d'objets précieux auxquels le maître de maison tient particulièrement.*
Ci-dessus, à gauche: *L'ovale qui surmonte le fauteuil abrite une curieuse collection de sceaux de cire.*
Ci-dessus, à droite: *un petit fauteuil de bambou dans une chambre à coucher. Le portrait dessiné a été réalisé par un artiste crémonois anonyme du 18e siècle.*

First pages, left: *Fattoria Le Fontanelle; a table decorated with two fabrics by Castellini seen through the door.*
First pages, right: *a marble mantelpiece with a small collection of porcelain balls, vessels and candleholders in which the colour blue predominates. On the wall are two ovals with 18th-century portraits from Piedmont.*
Previous pages: *the arched ceiling in the main living room is part of the villa's original structure. The furnishings are upholstered in a variety of fabrics but many are by the Milanese interior designer Mimma Gini. The matting is by Piero Castellini himself. Note the freedom of spirit that has guided selection of the furnishings, which are harmonized by the skilful use of colour.*

Facing page: *This outstanding cabinet in Chinese style holds a collection of Piero Castellini's books and other items with a significant commercial or sentimental value.*
Above left: *The oval frame above the chair holds an unusual collection of sealing wax.*
Above right: *a small bamboo chair in one of the bedrooms. The portrait on the wall is by an anonymous 18th-century artist from Cremona.*

Eingangsseiten, links: *die Fattoria Le Fontanelle; in der Türöffnung wird ein Tisch mit zwei Decken von Piero Castellini sichtbar.*
Eingangsseiten, rechts: *Auf dem marmornen Kaminsims befindet sich eine kleine, in Blau gehaltene Sammlung von Gefäßen, Flakons und Kerzenleuchtern aus Porzellan. Die oval gerahmten Reliefporträts sind piemontesische Arbeiten aus dem 18. Jahrhundert.*
Vorhergehende Doppelseite: *Die Gewölbedecke im Hauptwohnraum stammt noch aus der Entstehungszeit der »fattoria«. Die Möbel sind mit Stoffen unterschiedlicher Herkunft bezogen – viele stammen von der Mailänder Innenarchitektin Mimma Gini. Die Bodenmatten hat Piero Castellini selbst entworfen. Die einheitliche Farbgebung eint die frei kombinierten Möbel.*
Linke Seite: *In diesem außergewöhnlichen Möbelstück, einem Schrank im chinesischen Stil, verwahrt der Hausherr Bücher, wertvolle Objekte und Dinge, die ihm besonders ans Herz gewachsen sind.*
Oben links: *In dem ovalen Rahmen über dem Sessel befindet sich eine interessante Sammlung von Siegeln.*
Oben rechts: *ein zierlicher Bambusstuhl in einem der Schlafzimmer. Die Porträtzeichnung fertigte ein unbekannter Künstler aus Cremona im 18. Jahrhundert.*

Sous les nuages de vapeurs boriques de Larderello, une route bordée de cyprès remonte la Valle del Diavolo et mène au «casale» des Poggetti Alti. La bâtisse sobre a été construite de manière traditionnelle avec des pierres ramassées dans les champs des environs. Autrefois, on couchait au premier étage, au-dessus de la cuisine et de l'étable situées au rez-de-chaussée. Giancarlo et Maria Gloria Conti Bicocchi ont restauré le «casale» qui appartient aujourd'hui au fils de Maria Gloria, Stefano Isola, et à sa femme Matilde Gugliardo di Carpinello. Mais Poggetti Alti vit aussi à une époque vivre et travailler l'artiste Daniel Buren. Giancarlo et Maria Gloria ont tenu à conserver les encadrements des portes et des fenêtres, et les dallages d'origine. L'étable a été transformée avec beaucoup de goût en salle de séjour. A côté des anciennes mangeoires, des meubles du 19e siècle cohabitent parfaitement avec les créations dépouillées de Giancarlo Bicocchi.

Casale Poggetti Alti

Leave the marshlands of the Maremma along the Valle del Diavolo, skirting the boracic fumaroles of Larderello, and the cypress-lined road takes you to the farmhouse of Poggetti Alti. The stones used for the outer walls were found locally in the fields. Giancarlo and Maria Gloria Conti Bicocchi restructured the "casale" that belongs today to Maria Gloria's son, Stefano Isola, and to his wife, Matilde Gugliardo di Carpinello. But the artist Daniel Buren also lived here and left his mark. The doors, windows and floors have been left as they were and the rooms are still arranged as in the original plan; with the kitchen and stable, now a living room, on the ground floor and the bedrooms on the first floor. In the former stables, Giancarlo and Maria Gloria have created a strikingly stylish room: mangers and antique furniture contrast with other pieces whose spare lines were conceived by Giancarlo Bicocchi.

Die heißen Bordämpfe von Larderello liegen über der von Zypressen gesäumten Straße, die sich die Valle del Diavolo, das Teufelstal, hinaufwindet bis zum Casale Poggetti Alti. Der schlichte Gutshof wurde nach lokaler Tradition mit Felsbrocken errichtet, die die Bauern auf den umliegenden, steinigen Feldern sammelten. Damals schlief man im ersten Stock über der Küche und dem Stall. Zwischenzeitlich lebte und arbeitete in dem »casale« der Künstler Daniel Buren; heute wohnen hier Stefano Isola und seine Frau Matilde Gugliardo di Carpinello. Restauriert wurde Poggetti Alti von Stefanos Mutter Maria Gloria Conti Bicocchi und ihrem Mann Giancarlo Bicocchi. Bei der Restaurierung war ihnen wichtig, daß die alten Tür- und Fenstereinfassungen sowie die Fußböden erhalten blieben. Im ehemaligen Stall haben sie einen Wohnraum mit besonderem Flair eingerichtet: In dem Raum mit den original erhaltenen Futterkrippen fügen sich schnörkellose Entwürfe von Giancarlo Bicocchi gekonnt zwischen Möbeln des 19. Jahrhunderts ein.

Double page précédente, à gauche: la ferme, au sommet de la colline tournée vers les «balze», des escarpements près de Volterra; la pergola adossée au côté sud de la maison, avec une table conçue par Giancarlo Bicocchi et peinte par Daniel Buren.
Double page précédente, à droite: le corridor du premier étage qui dessert les chambres.
Ci-dessus, à gauche: Cette chambre à coucher renferme de vieux meubles de famille, dont une commode Empire et un lit en fer peint.
Ci-dessus, à droite: une autre chambre avec une coiffeuse du 19e siècle de bois clair et d'amarante.
Page de droite: une autre chambre au plafond peint en vert menthe et aux murs en rose, comme toutes les chambres du premier étage. Lit à baldaquin du 19e siècle avec son faîte en bois d'origine.

Previous pages, left: The "casale" on the hilltop looks out over the "balze", the crags of Volterra; the pergola on the southern side of the house with a table designed by Giancarlo Bicocchi and painted by Daniel Buren.
Previous pages, right: the corridor on the first floor with the bedrooms leading off.
Above left: a bedroom with antique furniture belonging to the family, including an Empire chest of drawers and a painted iron bed.
Above right: another bedroom with a 19th-century dressing table in natural wood and amaranth.
Facing page: The ceiling of all the rooms on the first floor is painted mint green and the walls pink. The wooden decoration on the canopy of the 19th-century, four-poster bed is original.

Vorhergehende Doppelseite, links: das Gehöft auf einem Hügel in der Nähe der »balze«, der steilen Abhänge von Volterra; die Pergola an der Südseite des Hauses mit einem Tisch, den Giancarlo Bicocchi entworfen und Daniel Buren lackiert hat.
Vorhergehende Doppelseite, rechts: Über diesen Flur erreicht man die Schlafzimmer im ersten Stock.
Oben links: ein Schlafzimmer mit alten Möbeln aus Familienbesitz, wie einer Empire-Truhe und einem Bett mit bemaltem Eisengestell.
Oben rechts: In einem weiteren Zimmer steht ein Toilettentisch aus dem 19. Jahrhundert aus hellem Holz und Amarantholz.
Rechte Seite: Alle Räume im ersten Geschoß haben eine mintgrün gestrichene Decke und rosafarbene Wände. Das Himmelbett aus dem 19. Jahrhundert besitzt noch die hölzerne Originalbekrönung.

Rita Foschi ne pouvait vraiment plus vivre en ville, à Rome. Elle s'est donc installée en Toscane avec sa famille, en pleine campagne, aux environs de Grosseto. Son mari s'occupe des terres, leur fils aîné va à l'université et le plus jeune l'aide dans sa nouvelle activité: elle s'est improvisée antiquaire, avec un certain succès. C'est de cette façon qu'elle a meublé la maison. «Mais – avoue-t-elle – il est toujours difficile de sélectionner ce que l'on veut vendre et ce que l'on désire conserver. Finalement, je garde ce qui va avec le style de la maison construite en 1863 et restaurée avec le plus grand soin». La cuisine est ainsi devenue un véritable musée des ustensiles de bois campagnards, recueillis avec amour dans toutes les régions d'Italie et de France, ainsi que les broderies, les cafetières françaises et les boîtes en fer-blanc peintes à la main.

Rita Foschi

Rita Foschi decided she could no longer put up with life in the city; so she, her husband and their two children left Rome for Tuscany, where they moved into a house in the countryside, near Grosseto. Rita's husband looks after the estate and her elder son is at university while the younger one gives her a hand with the new occupation she has taken up: dealing in antiques. This has enabled her to furnish the house, which was built in 1863. "But then it's always difficult," she confesses, "to know what to sell and what to hold on to. I end up by keeping whatever is in harmony with the spirit of the house, which we have restructured as faithfully as possible." The kitchen is a veritable museum of wooden implements used in the countryside, which come from all over Italy and France, as do her collections of embroidery, French coffee pots and hand-painted tins.

Eines Tages entschied Rita Foschi, daß sie nicht mehr in der Stadt leben wollte. Sie zog gemeinsam mit ihrem Mann und ihren beiden Söhnen von Rom in die Toskana und erwarb ein Haus auf dem Land, in der Nähe von Grosseto. Heute bearbeitet Ritas Mann die dazugehörigen Felder, der älteste Sohn studiert und der jüngere hilft der Mutter bei ihrer neuen Tätigkeit als erfolgreiche Antiquitätenhändlerin. Mit ihren »Fundstücken« hat sie auch das 1863 erbaute Haus eingerichtet. »Aber es ist für mich immer noch schwierig«, erzählt sie, »mich von meinen Stücken zu trennen. Ich gebe nichts her, was zum Stil unseres Hauses paßt. Bei der Restaurierung haben wir so weit wie möglich die ursprünglichen Strukturen bewahrt.« Die Küche mit dem rosettengeschmückten offenen Kamin gleicht einem Museum des bäuerlichen Lebens: sie quillt buchstäblich über von Holz- und Metallgerätschaften, die Rita aus ganz Italien und Frankreich zusammengetragen hat. Ihre Sammelleidenschaft gilt insbesondere Stickereien aller Art, französischen Kaffeekannen und handbemalten Blechdosen.

Page de gauche: Sur le meuble de mercerie on a rassemblé des bougies et divers objets, notamment, à gauche, un panier provençal. Une splendide collection de carrés d'essai, c'est-à-dire d'exemples de broderies destinés à l'apprentissage, orne ce mur.
Ci-dessus: La cuisine abrite une petite collection de boîtes en fer-blanc peintes à la main. Au mur, on peut voir des aquarelles et des gravures françaises aux motifs de poulets et de poules.
Double page suivante: la cuisine.

Facing page: Candles and other objects crowd the top of the sewing cupboard. A Provençal basket can be made out on the left. The wall is brightened up by a fine collection of samplers, or examples of needlework for would-be embroiderers.
Above: In the kitchen, there is a small collection of hand-painted 19th-century tins. French watercolours and engravings with chicken motifs adorn the walls.
Following pages: the immense kitchen.

Linke Seite: Auf der Nähkommode stehen Kerzen und andere Gegenstände, darunter auch ein ungewöhnlicher provenzalischer Korb. Die Wand schmücken Stickereien, die einst als Lehrmodelle dienten.
Oben: In der Küche befindet sich eine kleine Sammlung handbemalter Blechdosen aus dem 19. Jahrhundert. Verschiedene französische Aquarelle und Stiche mit Motiven aus dem Hühnerstall schmücken die Wand.
Folgende Doppelseite: die geräumige Küche.

A l'instar de nombreux Italiens, Horst Bauer et Jürgen Weiss consacrent le mois d'août à leurs vacances et à leur maison, située dans l'arrière-pays côtier aride. L'ancienne ferme devient alors le théâtre de succulentes expériences culinaires, relevées par les fines herbes aromatiques de leur potager. Ils ont fait montre d'une passion similaire quand ils ont restructuré le «casale», récupérant même de vieilles poutres et des arcs en granit d'origine. Ils ont modifié l'intérieur pour créer des espaces plus vastes et se sont efforcés de respecter le style traditionnel, en dissimulant les panneaux solaires avec soin. L'intérieur se veut résolument sobre, d'une élégance fine et discrète: «Il suffit d'un lit, d'une table et d'une chaise» — affirment les deux antiquaires de Munich, architectes d'intérieur confirmés. Cette profession de foi ne les a toutefois pas empêchés de dénicher des pièces originales et intéressantes pour leur maison, et ils continuent à prospecter la région avec enthousiasme, à la recherche de l'objet rare.

Horst Bauer
e Jürgen Weiss

As for many Italians, August is a holiday time for Horst Bauer and Jürgen Weiss — a time for their house in the sparse coastal hinterland. In the former farmhouse, they devote themselves to the creation of delicious dishes, experimenting with aromatic herbs from their own garden. They are antique dealers — with a shop in Munich — as well as expert interior designers. They brought a similar expertise to the restructuring of the "casale"; even finding authentic building materials, such as old beams for the ceilings and granite for the arches. They gutted the building so that they could redesign the interior and make larger rooms. Local traditions have been adhered to and the solar panels are carefully hidden from view. Inside there is an air of rarefied austerity: "A bed, a table and a chair are quite enough," assert the two antiquarians, who nevertheless continue to comb the open-air markets of the area in their search for interesting items.

Wie für viele Italiener sind die Augustwochen auch für Horst Bauer und Jürgen Weiss Ferienzeit — Zeit für ihr Haus im karg bewachsenen Hinterland der Küste. Der ehemalige Bauernhof wird dann zu einer Bühne, auf der sie sich dem Kreieren von köstlichen Gerichte hingeben. Dabei experimentieren sie mit aromatischen Kräutern aus dem eigenen Garten. Eine ähnliche Leidenschaft haben die beiden Münchener Antiquitätenhändler und erfahrenen Innenarchitekten auch bei der Umstrukturierung des »casale« bewiesen, für die sie sogar originale Deckenbalken und Granitbögen auftrieben. Zunächst wurde das Gebäude entkernt, um großzügigere Räumlichkeiten zu schaffen. Solarzellen wurden an unauffälligen Stellen angebracht, damit die Ursprünglichkeit des Hauses gewahrt blieb. Die schlichten Innenräume inszenierten die beiden mit feinem Gespür und vornehmer Zurückhaltung. »Ein Bett, ein Tisch und ein Stuhl reichen völlig aus«, lautet ihre Überzeugung. Trotzdem haben sie natürlich interessante und originelle Raritäten für ihr Heim gefunden — und sind auch weiterhin begeistert auf der Suche danach.

Double page précédente, à gauche: les deux antiquaires Jürgen Weiss et Horst Bauer; la galerie ouverte qui fait le tour de la ferme décorait autrefois l'église du village.
Double page précédente, à droite: la porte de bois massif de l'une des entrées de la ferme. Au-dessus des fauteuils néobaroques est accrochée une gouache de Serge Poliakoff (1906–1969). Les lourdes dalles de pierre de l'extérieur proviennent d'une ancienne rue villageoise.
Page de gauche: vue de la salle à manger et de la cuisine sur la salle où se trouve la cheminée. Au-dessus de la cheminée siennoise du 17e siècle, les cornes spiralées d'un élan. Au premier plan, un buste romain en marbre du 18e siècle. Les bas-reliefs médiévaux en marbre, au-dessus, représentent les signes zodiacaux des maîtres de maison.
Ci-dessus, à gauche: La ferme est sobrement meublée. Ici un tabouret à traire tout simple et une petite table en fer. L'aquarelle a été réalisée par le peintre allemand Horst Antes.
Ci-dessus, à droite: une chaise en fer française du tournant du siècle. A l'arrière-plan, on aperçoit une commode toulousaine avec une collection de céramiques rustiques régionales.

Previous pages, left: *the two antiquarians Jürgen Weiss and Horst Bauer; the portico around the farmhouse came from a village church.*
Previous pages, right: *one of the entrances to the farmhouse with a door of solid wood. Above the neo-Baroque armchairs hangs a gouache by Serge Poliakoff (1906–1969). The heavy stone slabs outside are from an old village street.*
Facing page: *looking from the dining-room and kitchen to the living room. Over the 17th-century Sienese fireplace are the horns of an eland. In the foreground is an 18th-century Roman bust in marble. The medieval marble reliefs above it represent the owners' signs of the zodiac.*

Above left: *Simplicity is one of the guiding principles of the house. Here, it is exemplified by a milking stool from the byre and a small iron table. The watercolour is by the German painter Horst Antes.*
Above right: *a French iron chair dating from the turn of the century. In the background is a chest of drawers from Toulouse, with a collection of rustic ceramic vessels made locally.*

Vorhergehende Doppelseite, links: *die beiden Antiquitätenhändler und Innenarchitekten Jürgen Weiss und Horst Bauer; der umlaufende Portikus des Bauernhauses schmückte einst eine Dorfkirche.*
Vorhergehende Doppelseite, rechts: *Durch einen Eingang mit massiver Holztür betritt man den Bauernhof. Über den neobarocken Sesseln hängt eine Gouache von Serge Poliakoff (1906–1969). Die schweren Steinplatten des Außenbereiches stammen von einer ehemaligen Dorfstraße.*
Linke Seite: *der Durchblick vom Eßraum und der Küche in den Kaminraum. Über dem sienesischen Kamin aus dem 17. Jahrhundert hängt das Geweih einer Elenantilope. Im Vordergrund sieht man eine römische Marmorbüste aus dem 18. Jahrhundert. Die mittelalterlichen Marmorreliefs darüber stellen die Tierkreiszeichen der Hausbesitzer dar.*
Oben links: *Der Bauernhof ist zurückhaltend möbliert. Hier ein einfacher Melkschemel aus dem Stall und ein kleiner Eisentisch. Das Aquarell ist ein Werk des deutschen Malers Horst Antes.*
Oben rechts: *ein französischer Eisenstuhl aus der Zeit der Jahrhundertwende. Im Hintergrund sieht man eine Kommode aus Toulouse mit einer Sammlung rustikaler Keramikgefäße aus der Region.*

Ci-dessus: Le sobre escalier en pierre qui mène aux chambres du premier étage faisait partie à l'origine d'une autre habitation et a été monté sur des supports de vieux rails de chemin de fer. Un dessin, un tableau et quelques objets anciens ornent l'espace au pavement de brique. Les chaises de paille sans prétention se trouvaient déjà dans la maison à l'arrivée de Horst Bauer et Jürgen Weiss.
Page de droite: Cette partie de la maison, qui s'ouvre sur la cage d'escalier, offre aussi un caractère dépouillé: un pavement de brique, une console française ornée d'une céramique napolitaine, une jarre en terre cuite. Au mur, les cornes d'un koudou.

Above: The staircase area of the house has a terracotta floor and is decorated with just a drawing, a painting and one or two antiques. The simple stone staircase itself leads up to the bedrooms on the first floor. It was originally from a different house and was built on old railway sleepers. The plain, straw-seated chairs were in the house when Horst Bauer and Jürgen Weiss took it over.
Facing page: This part of the house, opening onto the stairwell, is free of embellishment too: just a terracotta floor, a French console table with a Neapolitan ceramic vessel and a large earthenware jar. On the wall are the horns of a kudu.

Oben: Die einfache Steintreppe führt zu den Schlafzimmern im ersten Geschoß. Sie stammt ursprünglich aus einem anderen Haus und wurde auf Trägern von alten Eisenbahnschienen eingebaut. Die Wände schmücken eine Zeichnung, ein Gemälde und einige antike Stücke. Die schlichten Stühle mit Sitzen aus Strohgeflecht fanden Horst Bauer und Jürgen Weiss in dem Haus vor.
Rechte Seite: Auch dieser Teil des Hauses, der in das offene Treppenhaus übergeht, ist schnörkellos gehalten: Terrakotta-Fußboden, ein französischer Konsoltisch mit einem Keramikgefäß aus Neapel, ein Tonkrug. An der Wand hängt ein Kudugeweih.

Tuscany Interiors Horst Bauer e Jürgen Weiss

Page de gauche: Sous le portique, une table invite à se restaurer en plein air. La plaque de marbre repose sur le cadre d'un ancien lit de camp. Devant les deux vases néoclassiques, un arrangement de fleurs et de plantes odorantes. Les chaises italiennes en fer et rotin datent des années cinquante. La bougie est suspendue à l'intérieur d'un vase de verre qui la protège du vent.
Ci-dessus: La lumière pénètre dans la salle à manger par les deux portes à vantaux. Les deux bancs de bois se trouvaient à l'origine dans un ancien couvent. Le dossier au premier plan est celui d'un fauteuil paysan catalan.
A droite: la cuisine, centre des exploits gastronomiques. Design et technique modernes contrastent volontairement avec la salle à manger rustique.

Facing page: Beneath the portico is an inviting table for alfresco meals. The marble top rests on an old military bedstead. In front of the neoclassical vases is a still life of flowers and herbs. The Italian iron and cane chairs date from the Fifties; the candle above is hanging in a glass shade to protect it from the wind.
Above: The light floods into the dining room through the French doors. The two wooden benches are from a former monastery. The chair-back in the foreground belongs to a Catalonian farmhouse chair.
Right: the kitchen, where fabulous meals are created. Modern design and technology are in deliberate contrast to the rustic dining-room.

Linke Seite: Unter dem Portikus lädt ein Tisch zum Essen im Freien ein. Die Marmorplatte ruht auf dem Gestell eines ehemaligen Militärbettes. Vor den beiden klassizistischen Vasen ist ein Stilleben aus Blumen und Kräutern arrangiert. Die italienischen Stühle aus Eisen und Rohrgeflecht stammen aus den fünfziger Jahren.

Oben: Durch die Flügeltüren flutet Licht in das Eßzimmer. Die beiden Holzbänke stammen aus einem ehemaligen Kloster. Die Lehne im Vordergrund gehört zu einem katalanischen Bauernstuhl.
Rechts: die Küche, Ort der gastronomischen Sternstunden. Zeitgenössisches Design und moderne Technik stehen bewußt im Kontrast zum rustikalen Eßraum.

Des chiens et des chats, des sangliers et autres animaux des bois, sans parler d'un tigre apprivoisé, peuplent le vaste domaine qui entoure la Villa Olmaia dans la Maremme de Livourne. Bâti sur les ruines de la Villa Serristori détruite au cours de la dernière guerre, l'édifice conçu par l'architecte Tullio Rossi en 1957 se fond dans la nature environnante et exalte l'esprit des lieux qui embrasa l'âme de Gabriele D'Annunzio – il écrivit à Marina di Pisa, «La mort du cerf», dont trois vers sont gravés au-dessus de l'entrée de la villa: «On entendait au loin la mer – accompagner de son grondement – le murmure des bois.» La Villa Olmaia est ouverte de tous côtés au soleil et au vent venu de la mer toute proche; ils la traversent sans entrave et y insufflent la chaleur et les parfums d'une terre sauvage, celle de l'ancienne Maremme du temps où sévissait la malaria.

Villa Olmaia

Dogs, cats, wild boar and a host of other animals – including a pet tiger – live on the huge estate of Villa Olmaia in the Leghorn Maremma area, built on the ruins of the former Villa Serristori that was destroyed during the last war. Designed by the architect Tullio Rossi in 1957, Villa Olmaia merges seamlessly into the surrounding countryside and is pervaded by a "genius loci" that fired the soul of Gabriele D'Annunzio, who wrote "Death of a Stag" at Marina di Pisa. Three of its verses are inscribed over the entrance of Villa Olmaia: "Faint could be heard the sea – echoing in its roar – the whispers of the woods". The villa is exposed on all sides to sunshine from dawn till dusk. It is also swept by breezes from the shore that blow freely through the rooms, bringing with them the heat and perfumes of the untamed Maremma of yesteryear, still as pungent as they were in the days when malaria ravaged the territory.

Wildschweine, Hunde, Katzen und ein gezähmter Tiger bevölkern das weitläufige Grundstück der Villa Olmaia. Das Anwesen entstand 1957 auf den Ruinen der im Zweiten Weltkrieg zerstörten Villa Serristori. Der Architekt Tullio Rossi hat es verstanden, die Villa harmonisch in die wilde Küstenlandschaft der Maremma Livornese einzufügen, die schon Gabriele d'Annunzio begeisterte. Die Inschrift über dem Eingang ist ein Zitat aus seinem Gedicht »Der Tod des Hirschen«, das in Marina di Pisa entstand: »Und von Fern' ertönte des Meeres Brausen / Im Gleichklang mit der Wälder Wispern«. Nach allen Seiten öffnet sich die Villa der ungezähmten Landschaft: dem gleißenden Sonnenlicht, der Wärme und den unverkennbaren Gerüchen der Maremma.

Double page précédente, à gauche: le patio de la Villa Olmaia, orné d'une bignone grimpante; la plage privée.
Double page précédente, à droite: le vestiaire des chasseurs.
A droite: une paroi de la salle à manger ornée, à la manière toscane, d'assiettes de la série «Tulipano» de Richard Ginori.
Ci-dessous: le vaste séjour avec sa voûte légèrement incurvée. Les meubles d'époques diverses proviennent de différentes demeures. Aux murs, on peut voir des tableaux animaliers, des portraits et des trophées de chasse.

Previous pages, left: the patio at Villa Olmaia, shaded by an exotic bignonia; the villa's private beach.
Previous pages, right: the hunters' changing room.
Right: One wall in the dining room has been decorated in the Tuscan manner with plates from Richard Ginori's "Tulipano" series.
Below: the generously proportioned living room with its characteristic, gently curving vault. The furniture comes from a number of different sources and periods. Pictures of animals, portraits and hunting trophies decorate the walls.

Vorhergehende Doppelseite, links: Eine Bignonie beschattet den Innenhof der Villa Olmaia; der Privatstrand.
Vorhergehende Doppelseite, rechts: das Ankleidezimmer der Jäger.
Rechts: typisch toskanischer Wandschmuck im Speisezimmer – Teller der Serie »Tulipano« von Richard Ginori.
Unten: der geräumige Wohnraum mit dem charakteristischen, flachen Gewölbe. Die Möbel stammen aus unterschiedlichen Epochen und Häusern. An den Wänden finden sich Tierdarstellungen, Porträts und Jagdtrophäen.

Ci-dessus: le hall d'entrée, où deux chiens semblent monter la garde.
Les défenses d'éléphant proviennent du Kenya. Par l'embrasure de la
porte, on entrevoit une pièce conçue pour lire ou regarder la télévision
et qui s'ouvre au fond sur le séjour.
A droite: une tête-trophée de buffle, souvenir d'Afrique.

Above: The two dogs snoozing in the entrance area look as if they are
keeping one eye open for new arrivals. The elephant tusks are from
Kenya. A room for reading or watching television can be seen through
the doorway, and beyond that the main living room.
Right: a buffalo-head hunting trophy from an African safari.

Oben: Die beiden Hunde scheinen den Eingangsbereich des Hauses
zu bewachen. Die Elefantenstoßzähne stammen aus Kenia. Durch
die Türöffnung blickt man in das Lese- und Fernsehzimmer, an das
sich im Hintergrund der Wohnraum anschließt.
Rechts: der Kopf eines Büffels – eine Jagdtrophäe aus Afrika.

Ci-dessus: Dans un angle de la salle à manger, on peut voir un portrait réalisé par le peintre italien Pietro Annigoni.
Page de droite: Cette chambre abrite un lit à colonnes de bois façonnées au tour, datant du 19e siècle.

Above: A portrait painted by the Italian artist Pietro Annigoni hangs in one corner of the dining room.
Facing page: one of the bedrooms. The bed with turned-wood posts dates from the 19th century.

Oben: Das Porträt im Speisezimmer stammt von dem Maler Pietro Annigoni.
Rechte Seite: ein Schlafzimmer. Das Bett mit gedrechselten Holzpfosten entstand im 19. Jahrhundert.

Pisa e dintorni

En 1821, le poète anglais Lord Byron dut se réfugier en Toscane. Il loua l'un des plus beaux palais de Pise, le Palazzo Lanfranchi, au bord de l'Arno, qui jouxtait la maison de son ami, le poète Percy Bysshe Shelley. Sa demeure devint vite un foyer d'agitation révolutionnaire très surveillé par la police du grand-duché. Les tracasseries policières, l'expulsion de sa maîtresse Teresa Gamba Guiccioli et la mort de Shelley en mer incitèrent Byron à quitter Pise dès 1822. Après avoir plusieurs fois changé de mains, le palais échut aux Toscanelli qui chargèrent l'architecte Alessandro Gherardesca de le restructurer. L'intérieur est décoré d'allégories liées à la musique. Ses muses perdues dans un ciel de lapis-lazuli et d'or sont maintenant en partie cachées par des rayonnages chargés de documents. Car depuis le début du siècle le Palazzo Toscanelli abrite les Archives d'Etat.

Lord Byron

When the English poet Lord Byron came to Pisa as an exile, he rented one of the loveliest buildings in the city, Palazzo Lanfranchi on the Lungarno embankment, near the house where his friend Percy Bysshe Shelley was living. The palazzo soon became a meeting place for romantics and revolutionaries, and was kept under close watch by the Grand Duke of Lorraine's police. The consequent harassment, the expulsion from the Grand Duchy of his lover, Teresa Gamba Guiccioli, and Shelley's death by drowning brought Byron's stay in Pisa to an end. The palazzo then changed hands several times before the Toscanellis commissioned the architect Alessandro Gherardesca to make extensive renovations. The decoration is inspired by allegorical, art-related themes. The muses look down from a lapis lazuli and gold sky or lie half-hidden behind the documents that line the time-worn shelves, for Palazzo Toscanelli has been the home of the State Archive since the turn of the century.

Der von der englischen Gesellschaft geächtete Dichter Lord Byron floh nach Pisa und mietete eines der schönsten Gebäude der Stadt, den Palazzo Lanfranchi. Dieser lag am Arnoufer direkt neben dem Haus seines Freundes, des Dichters Percy Bysshe Shelley. Die neue Bleibe entwickelte sich rasch zu einem beliebten Treffpunkt, den die lothringische Polizei überwachte. Als seine Geliebte Teresa Gamba Guiccioli aus dem Großherzogtum ausgewiesen wurde und Shelley im Meer ertrank, verließ Byron Pisa. In der Folge wechselten die Eigentümer des Palazzo häufig, bis das Gebäude im 19. Jahrhundert in den Besitz der Familie Toscanelli gelangte. Sie betraute mit dem Umbau den Architekten Alessandro Gherardesca. Die Innendekorationen bestehen aus allegorischen Darstellungen der Musik unter einem eindrucksvollen Himmel aus Lapislazuli und Gold. Heute lugen die Musen zwischen alten Regalen hervor, denn seit Beginn des 20. Jahrhunderts beherbergt Palazzo Toscanelli das Staatsarchiv.

Les architectes Massimo et Gabriella Ioli Carmassi ont aménagé leur demeure et leur studio avec une terrasse ombragée par des glycines dans un vieux bâtiment de Pise issu de la restructuration de «case a torre» au 18e siècle. Ils se passionnent pour la réhabilitation d'édifices anciens profondément transformés au cours des siècles, cherchant à fondre leur intervention dans l'ensemble afin que le résultat final présente la même harmonie que l'édifice d'origine. Ils accordent donc une extrême importance aux détails, aux finitions, aux dallages, aux encadrements des portes et des fenêtres et manifestent un grand respect pour la structure de l'édifice. Ils utilisent des technologies et des matériaux très légers, comme des escaliers de métal en colimaçon, qui laissent passer la lumière, ou des bois clairs. L'ouverture des portes autrefois murées offre de nouvelles perspectives.

Massimo e Gabriella Ioli Carmassi

Massimo and Gabriella Ioli Carmassi's house and studio in Pisa are in a building that was created during the 18th century from medieval "case a torre". An ancient wistaria shades the terrace behind. The couple's professional activities as architects are mainly concerned with restructuring heavily layered buildings. "It is not easy," maintain Massimo and Gabriella, "to add the final layer so that it will preserve the building's original quality." Here, detail is all-important. Care is taken over fixtures, floors, doors and windows. Inside, the house is divided up using airy technologies and materials, such as open metal spiral staircases and natural wood. Doors closed off long ago have been unbricked and, flanked now by other apertures, create fresh perspectives, bringing the internal spaces together in exciting new configurations.

Das Gebäude, in dem Massimo und Gabriella Ioli Carmassi leben und arbeiten, entstand im 18. Jahrhundert. Damals wurden mehrere »case a torre« zu einem Gesamtkomplex zusammengefaßt und an der Rückseite eine glyzinienbeschattete Terrasse angelegt. Die beiden Architekten sind Spezialisten für die Restaurierung historischer Gebäude mit wechselvoller Baugeschichte. »Die letzten Veränderungen – also diejenigen, die wir vornehmen – müssen mit den vorhergehenden harmonieren«, stellen sie fest. Wie bei vielen anderen einfühlsam restaurierten Häusern legten Massimo und Gabriella auch bei diesem Gebäudeverbund besonderen Wert auf die originalen Fußböden sowie Tür- und Fenstereinfassungen, da diese den Charakter des Hauses wesentlich mitbestimmen. Die äußere Erscheinung erfuhr keinerlei Veränderung; bei der Innenausstattung verwendeten sie helle, moderne und leichte Materialien, die die Räume mit Licht erfüllen. Nachdem zugemauerte Türen freigelegt worden waren, entstanden neue Durchblicke und eindrucksvolle Raumverbindungen.

Double page précédente, à gauche: Massimo et Gabriella Ioli Carmassi; le plafond du salon orné par le peintre pisan Giovanni Battista Tempesti (1732-1802); l'escalier à vis en métal.
Double page précédente, à droite: La terrasse, à l'arrière de la maison, est aménagée pour passer d'agréables moments de détente sous les glycines.
Ci-dessus et à droite: l'escalier en colimaçon et les structures de verre dépoli et de cuivre qui dissimulent la cuisine et la salle de bain.
Page de droite: L'espace de l'ancienne remise a été subdivisé. Les murs de verre donnent à la pièce transparence et clarté. Les deux chaises «B302» sont une création du célèbre Le Corbusier, datant de 1928/29. Sur le mur du fond, on peut voir une photographie de Massimo Carmassi.

Previous pages, left: Massimo and Gabriella Ioli Carmassi; the Pisan painter Giovanni Battista Tempesti (1732–1802) frescoed the ceiling in the main reception room; the metal spiral staircase.
Previous pages, right: the terrace behind the house where a moment's peace and quiet can be enjoyed under the shade of the wistaria.
Above and right: the spiral staircase and the structure in frosted glass and brass that masks the kitchen and bathroom.
Facing page: the room with an intermediate floor, inserted into what used to be the coach house. Glass walls lend transparency and clarity to the room. The two chairs, "B302" (1928/29), are by Le Corbusier. A photograph of Massimo Carmassi hangs on the far wall.

Vorhergehende Doppelseite, links: Massimo und Gabriella Ioli Carmassi; die zentrale Deckenmalerei des Salons; die Wendeltreppe aus Metall.
Vorhergehende Doppelseite, rechts: Glyzinien beschatten die Terrasse an der Rückseite der Villa – eine Oase der Ruhe.

Oben und rechts: die Wendeltreppe und die Konstruktion aus Milchglas und Messing, hinter der sich Küche und Bad verbergen.
Rechte Seite: In der ehemaligen Kutschenremise ist ein Raum mit eingezogenem Hängeboden entstanden. Wände aus Glas geben dem Raum Transparenz und Klarheit. Die beiden Stühle »B302« entwarf Le Corbusier 1928/29. An der Stirnwand hängt eine Fotografie von Massimo Carmassi.

Page de gauche: le bureau d'étude des deux architectes.
Ci-dessus: Le grand séjour du premier étage, au plafond orné de
fresques du peintre pisan Giovanni Battista Tempesti (1732–1802), est
entièrement garni de bibliothèques. Les canapés «grand confort» sont
une création de Le Corbusier datant de 1928. Au fond, un piano à
queue.
A droite: les tables de travail dans les studios de Massimo et Gabriella Ioli Carmassi. Ces pièces comportent également des fresques
du 19e siècle.

Facing page: the designers' room.
Above: The main living room on the first floor is generously furnished
with bookcases. The frescoes on the ceiling are by the Pisan painter
Giovanni Battista Tempesti (1732–1802). Le Corbusier chairs "Grand
Confort" (1928) stand in front of the fireplace and there is a grand
piano on the far side of the room.
Right: the work tables in Massimo and Gabriella Ioli Carmassi's
studios. These rooms were also frescoed in the 19th century.

Linke Seite: In diesem Raum arbeiten die beiden Architekten an
ihren Entwurfsplänen.
Oben: Das geräumige Wohnzimmer im ersten Geschoß beherbergt
zahlreiche Bücherregale. An der Decke prunken Fresken des pisani-
schen Malers Giovanni Battista Tempesti (1732–1802). Vor dem
Kamin stehen die Sessel »Grand Confort«, die Le Corbusier 1928
entwarf. Im Hintergrund sieht man einen Flügel.
Rechts: zwei Ansichten der Studios von Massimo und Gabriella Ioli
Carmassi mit Arbeitstischen. Auch diese Räume schmücken Fresken
aus dem 19. Jahrhundert.

La Villa Roncioni, à Pugnano di Pisa, a vu naître l'amour du jeune écrivain romantique Ugo Foscolo pour Isabella, qui lui inspirera en 1802 son roman intitulé «Les dernières lettres de Jacopo Ortis» dans la tradition du «Werther» de Goethe. La villa appartient toujours à la famille Roncioni et a conservé son aspect d'origine. Au centre de la façade, la porte d'entrée est surmontée d'une porte-fenêtre donnant sur un petit balcon; le tout est couronné du blason de la famille. Le jardin qui entoure la villa abrite un temple de Bacchus, un nymphée orné de rocailles. Mais le plus extraordinaire est le salon central de la villa, décoré par Giovanni Battista Tempesti de fresques en trompe-l'œil représentant un vaste portique avec colonnes, grands escaliers et balustrades.

Villa Roncioni

At Villa Roncioni, in Pugnano near Pisa, the young romantic poet Ugo Foscolo fell in love with Isabella, the inspiration of his novel "The Last Letters of Jacopo Ortis" of 1802 (the account of an unrequited love in the tradition of Goethe's "Sorrows of Young Werther"). The villa still belongs to the Roncioni family, who have conserved its original appearance. A graceful main entrance is surmounted by a window with a small balcony, itself surmounted by the family crest. The garden around the villa contains a number of constructions like the Temple of Bacchus, a nymphaeum decorated with scroll ornaments. It is, however, the interior of the villa that is truly extraordinary. The main living room, for instance, was frescoed by Giovanni Battista Tempesti with a "trompe-l'œil" that depicts a delicate colonnade, complete with pillars and banistered flights of stairs.

Die Liebe zu Isabella, einer der Damen des Hauses, inspirierte den jungen Dichter Ugo Foscolo 1802 zu dem romantischen Roman »Die letzten Briefe des Jacopo Ortis«, der in der Tradition von Goethes »Werther« eine unglückliche Liebe beschreibt. Auch heute noch ist das Herrenhaus in Pugnano, einem Dorf bei Pisa, im Besitz der Familie Roncioni. Ein kleiner, vom Familienwappen bekrönter Balkon über dem Eingangsportal mildert die Strenge des Gebäudes. Im Garten, der die streng wirkende Villa mit dem aufragenden Mittelbau umgibt, ist ein reich mit Muschelwerk verziertes Nymphäum zu bestaunen. Unerwartetes findet sich auch in den Innenräumen: In dem zentral gelegenen Salon glaubt man sich zunächst vor einem weitläufigen Bogengang mit zierlichen Säulen, Treppen und Balustraden. Doch es handelt sich um ein Fresko von Giovanni Battista Tempesti, der eine Scheinarchitektur kunstvoll auf die Wände bannte.

Page de gauche: le salon de musique. Les fresques de la fin du 18e siècle sont attribuées à Giuseppe Bacchini. Elles illustrent des thèmes mythologiques comme les «Noces de Bacchus et Ariane», «Ariane à Naxos» et le «Silène ivre».
Ci-dessus: le salon d'Isabella, un amour de Foscolo. Les fresques en trompe-l'œil du début du 19e siècle qui représentent des tentures et des bas-reliefs monochromes sont attribuées à Antonio Niccolini.
A droite: un autre aspect du salon d'Isabella, avec ses divans et ses fauteuils disposés autour de la cheminée.

Facing page: the music room. The late 18th-century frescoes are attributed to Giuseppe Bacchini and depict mythological themes: "The Marriage of Bacchus and Ariadne", "Ariadne on Naxos", and "The Drunkenness of Silenus".
Above: The room where Foscolo's inamorata, Isabella, received her guests. The "trompe-l'œil" frescoes of curtains and fake black and white bas-reliefs from the early 19th century are thought to be by Antonio Niccolini.
Right: another view of Isabella's sitting room, showing sofas and armchairs arranged around the fireplace.

Linke Seite: das Musikzimmer. Die Ende des 18. Jahrhunderts entstandenen Fresken werden Giuseppe Bacchini zugeschrieben. Sie zeigen mythologische Themen wie »Die Hochzeit von Bacchus und Ariadne«, »Ariadne auf Naxos« und »Der trunkene Silen«.
Oben: der Salon jener Isabella, an die Foscolo sein Herz verlor. Die »Trompe-l'œil«-Vorhänge sowie die täuschend echt wirkenden monochromen Flachreliefs stammen aus den ersten Jahren des 19. Jahrhunderts und wurden vermutlich von Antonio Niccolini geschaffen.
Rechts: In Isabellas Salon gruppieren sich Sofas und Sessel um den Kamin.

Page de gauche: La voûte située en haut des escaliers a été somp-
tueusement décorée de fresques par le peintre napolitain Pasquale
Cioffi en 1781. La balustrade de fer forgé entoure un double divan de
milieu.
Ci-dessus: Ce petit salon de la fin du 18e siècle a été décoré de paysages imaginaires vus à travers des voilages transparents en partie
soulevés, peints en trompe-l'œil, probablement par Giuseppe
Bacchini.

Facing page: The vault of the stairwell was sumptuously frescoed in a
"trompe-l'œil" perspective by the Neapolitan painter Pasquale Cioffi
in 1781. The wrought-iron banister provides an attractive setting for a
back-to-back double sofa.
Above: a small, late 18th-century sitting room decorated in "trompe-
l'œil", probably by Giuseppe Bacchini, with imaginary landscapes
glimpsed through diaphanous, partially drawn curtains.

Linke Seite: das Treppenhaus. Die prunkvollen Fresken, die die Tie-
fenwirkung des Gewölbes noch steigern, schuf der neapolitanische
Maler Pasquale Cioffi im Jahr 1781. Hinter der schmiedeeisernen
Brüstung steht ein Rundsofa.
Oben: ein kleiner Salon aus dem späten 18. Jahrhundert. Die phan-
tasievollen Landschaften hinter hauchdünnen, zurückgezogenen
»Trompe-l'œil«-Vorhängen stammen vermutlich von Giuseppe
Bacchini.

Cette villa a été construite à l'aube du 20e siècle par les Siemens, célèbres magnats allemands, qui recherchaient un endroit calme et sain. Le cadre les avait attirés par son atmosphère vaguement décadente et dionysiaque, pleine de réminiscences étrusques. Madame Siemens se faisait peindre nue sur la plage avec ses enfants, notamment par un de leurs invités, l'artiste allemand Adolf von Hildebrand (1847–1921). Après le départ des Siemens, la villa fut abandonnée. Puis, dans les années quatre-vingt, elle a connu une véritable résurrection grâce à la restauration minutieuse menée par Alfredo Forti. Pour la meubler, il a choisi des objets de la fin du 18e siècle, comme la bibliothèque néoclassique marquée par l'influence des gravures du Piranèse, du 19e siècle, comme la console néogothique noire, et des premières décennies du 20e siècle.

Villa Apuana

This villa has an intriguing history. It was built at the turn of the century for the Siemens family, who came in search of privacy and healthy air to these verdant pine groves on a sea once sailed by the Etruscans. They found what they were looking for in the villa's vaguely decadent, Dionysiac surroundings. The wife of the German industrialist had herself portrayed nude on the beach with her children, and another likeness, equally nude, was painted by her guest Adolf von Hildebrand (1847–1921), a German artist. When the family left, the villa remained empty. Its fortunes improved again in the Eighties when restoration work began under Alfredo Forti, who also selected the furnishings dating from the 18th century to the early years of the 20th century. He chose items such as a neoclassical bookcase redolent of the engravings of Giovanni Battista Piranesi and a neo-Gothic, black console table.

Diese faszinierende Villa im Schatten von Pinienwäldern wurde für die Familie von Siemens erbaut. Hier erschuf die deutsche Magnatenfamilie zu Beginn des Jahrhunderts ihre eigene, dekadent-dionysische Welt. Frau von Siemens ließ sich zusammen mit ihren Kindern nackt am Strand malen, und auch ihr Gast, der deutsche Künstler Adolf von Hildebrand (1847–1921), schuf seinerzeit einen Akt von ihr. Als die von Siemens gingen, versank die Villa in einen Dornröschenschlaf. Erst die umsichtige Restaurierung von Alfredo Forti in den achtziger Jahren erweckte sie zu neuem Leben. Forti trug auch die Inneneinrichtung zusammen. So kombinierte er gekonnt einen klassizistischen Bücherschrank aus dem späten 18. Jahrhundert, der an die Stiche Giovanni Battista Piranesis erinnert, mit einem schwarzen neugotischen Konsoltisch und Möbeln aus dem frühen 20. Jahrhundert.

Double page précédente, à gauche: la façade de la villa; la salle à manger est meublée d'une longue table, de sièges Thonet «n°14» et d'un lustre dessiné par Alfredo Forti.

Double page précédente, à droite: Le séjour est meublé d'un divan produit en série, à côté duquel est placée une petite table en rotin, identique à celle qui se trouve entre les deux fenêtres. Sur la table derrière le divan, on peut voir un curieux chandelier aux alvéoles remplies d'eau et une vitrine abritant un flamant rose empaillé. Les deux lustres sont signés Alfredo Forti.

Ci-dessus: Les deux lits à baldaquin en fer proviennent d'un couvent de religieuses et datent du début du 19e siècle.

Page de droite: La salle de bain revêtue de marbre et au plafond à treillage de bois a été conçue par Alfredo Forti.

Previous pages, left: the main façade of the villa; the dining room is furnished with a long table and Thonet chairs "No. 14". The chandelier was designed by Alfredo Forti.

Previous pages, right: The living room décor features a standard production sofa complemented by a wicker table similar to the one standing between the two windows. The light from the unusual lamp on the table behind the sofa is attenuated by water-filled spheres. Next to it stands a stuffed flamingo in a display case. Both lamps were designed by Alfredo Forti.

Above: The two iron tester beds came from a convent. They were made in the early 19th century.

Facing page: The marble-clad bathroom was designed by Alfredo Forti, who also conceived the wood-strip latticework decoration on the ceiling.

Vorhergehende Doppelseite, links: die Fassade der Villa; das Speisezimmer ist mit Thonet-Stühlen »Nr. 14« und einem von Alfredo Forti entworfenen Leuchter ausgestattet.

Vorhergehende Doppelseite, rechts: der Wohnraum. Neben dem Sofa und zwischen den beiden Fenstern stehen zierliche Tische aus Weidengeflecht. Auf dem Tisch rechts befinden sich ein interessanter Kerzenleuchter mit wassergefüllten Kugeln und ein Vitrinenaufsatz mit einem ausgestopften Flamingo. Die beiden Deckenleuchten sind ein Entwurf von Alfredo Forti.

Oben: zwei Himmelbetten mit eisernen Baldachingestellen. Sie stammen aus dem frühen 19. Jahrhundert und standen einst in einem Nonnenkloster.

Rechte Seite: Alfredo Forti gestaltete auch das Marmorbad. Die Decke schmückte er mit schmalen Holzleisten, die ein dekoratives Gitterwerk bilden.

La Lucchesia

Paolo Guinigi, «signore» de Lucques entre 1400 et 1430, a fait édifier en 1418 le Palazzo Pierantoni, le premier grand édifice de la Renaissance de la ville. On y accède par un atrium depuis lequel un grand escalier mène au «piano nobile». Là, un vaste salon occupe tout l'espace compris entre la façade et l'arrière du bâtiment. Au premier étage, on trouve partout des murs peints en faux bois, des pavements décorés, des stucs, des festons et des frises en trompe-l'œil. L'ameublement très éclectique comporte des chaises tapissées de soie ancienne de facture lucquoise, des commodes vénitiennes du 18e siècle, des portraits de famille, des natures mortes et des tableaux grandioses; enfin, une salle de bains ajoutée dans les années trente, ornée de citations grecques, répond à une chambre à coucher meublée en style pompéien.

Palazzo Pierantoni

The first major building to be erected in Lucca after the medieval era was the one built in 1418 by Paolo Guinigi, who was "Signore", or ruler, of Lucca. Today it is known as Palazzo Pierantoni. Entry is through a hall with a great staircase leading up to the "piano nobile". A spacious reception room occupies the entire depth of the building from the façade to the rear. Throughout the first floor, the walls are painted in a simulated wood effect, and there is a wealth of stuccos, festoons and "trompe-l'œil" friezes. The furnishings bear witness to a notable eclecticism of taste. Chairs upholstered in old Luccan silk stand next to 18th-century Venetian dressers, and family portraits rub shoulders with still lifes and old masters. One of the bedrooms has been decorated in a style inspired by Pompeii, and a bathroom installed in the Thirties flaunts a décor incorporating Greek inscriptions.

Paolo Guinigi, »signore« von Lucca, ließ 1418 den ersten bedeutenden neuzeitlichen Palazzo der Stadt errichten. Das heute als Palazzo Pierantoni bekannte Gebäude verfügt über ein Atrium, von dem eine prachtvolle Treppe in das »piano nobile« führt, dessen Wände aufwendig in Holznachbildung bemalt sind. Hier liegt auch ein Salon von riesigen Ausmaßen, der sich über die gesamte Tiefe des Gebäudes erstreckt. Staunend wandert der Blick über reiche Stuckverzierungen, gemalte, prächtige Girlanden und Friese in »Trompe-l'œil«-Technik. An den Wänden prunken Familienporträts und Stilleben Alter Meister. Neben venezianischen Kommoden des 18. Jahrhunderts stehen Stühle, die mit alten, in Lucca gefertigten Seidenstoffen bezogen sind. Jeder Raum hat seinen eigenen eklektizistischen Charme, das Schlafzimmer im »pompejanischen Stil« ebenso wie das mit griechischen Zitaten geschmückte Badezimmer aus den dreißiger Jahren.

Double page précédente, à gauche: l'extérieur du Palazzo Pierantoni; une commode du 18e siècle.
Double page précédente, à droite: l'escalier monumental qui mène à l'étage noble.
Ci-dessus, à gauche: Ce salon présente une cheminée de marbre de Carrare, des portraits de famille, des natures mortes, un lampadaire en cristal de Murano, des sièges de facture lucquoise et un plafond orné de stuc doré.
Ci-dessus, à droite: Dans la salle à manger richement décorée, des sièges de facture lucquoise jouxtent des meubles vénitiens. Le plafond de cette salle est aussi orné de stuc doré.
Page de droite: Les murs et le plafond du salon central sont richement décorés de stuc doré. On remarque un lampadaire en cristal de Murano, des fauteuils et des meubles de différentes époques.

Previous pages, left: the exterior of Palazzo Pierantoni; an 18th-century chest of drawers.
Previous pages, right: the great staircase leading up to the first floor.
Above left: a drawing room with fireplace in Carrara marble, family portraits, still lifes, a glass chandelier from Murano, silks from Lucca and a gilt stucco ceiling.
Above right: The sumptuous dining-room décor brings together locally made chairs and furniture from Venice under a gilt stucco ceiling.
Facing page: Walls and ceiling of the main reception room are richly decorated with gilt stucco. The chandelier is in Murano glass. Under the painting dating from the 18th century, chairs and furniture from a number of different periods.

Vorhergehende Doppelseite, links: die Fassade des Palazzo Pierantoni; eine Kommode aus dem 18. Jahrhundert.
Vorhergehende Doppelseite, rechts: Die monumentale Treppe führt hinauf zum Hauptgeschoß.
Oben links: der kleine Salon mit einem Kamin aus Carrara-Marmor, Familienporträts, Stilleben und einem Leuchter aus venezianischem Muranoglas. Die Sitzmöbel aus dem 18. Jahrhundert sind mit in Lucca gefertigten Seidenstoffen bezogen.
Oben rechts: Im opulent ausgestatteten Eßzimmer finden sich Stühle aus Lucca neben Möbelstücken aus Venedig. Die Decke schmücken Dekorationen aus vergoldetem Stuck.
Rechte Seite: Auch der zentral gelegene Salon mit dem Kristallüster aus Murano ist an Wänden und Decke reich mit vergoldetem Stuck verziert. Vor dem Gemälde aus dem 18. Jahrhundert gruppieren sich Sitzgelegenheiten aus verschiedenen Jahrhunderten.

La romancière Francesca Duranti habite cette demeure baptisée Villa Rossi, du nom de son père, Paolo Rossi, qui l'acheta peu de temps avant la Seconde Guerre mondiale. Francesco Burlamacchi (1498–1548), un célèbre politicien et opposant aux Médicis, fit édifier la villa décorée d'arcades au 16e siècle. Par la suite, elle changea souvent de propriétaires. L'un d'eux, un Hollandais ami de Napoléon III, y apporta les grands portraits officiels qui trônent encore dans la salle à manger donnant sur la loggia. Un Lucquois, don Lorenzo Altieri, épousa la pupille du Hollandais et la villa lui revint. Francesca Duranti adore cette demeure où elle a passé son enfance. Elle y est revenue après avoir longtemps vécu ailleurs. Le cadre paisible accroît le charme de la villa: d'un côté, une colline érige une muraille de verdure protectrice, de l'autre, une pelouse inclinée descend jusqu'à un étang où poussent de délicates fleurs de lotus.

Francesca Duranti

This villa is the home of the novelist Francesca Duranti, and is known as Villa Rossi after her father, Paolo Rossi, who bought it just before the Second World War. The original building, begun by Francesco Burlamacchi (1498–1548), a statesman and famous opponent of the Medici family, dates from the 16th century. Since then, however, the villa has had a number of owners, including a Dutchman who was intimate with the French Emperor Napoleon III and who brought with him the imposing court portraits that still dominate the dining room opening onto the portico. The property then passed to Don Lorenzo Altieri of Lucca on his marriage to a Russian princess, ward of the Dutch owner. Francesca Duranti is deeply attached to this villa, where she spent her childhood and where she has come back to settle after many years spent living elsewhere. But Villa Rossi also has other attractions. The countryside round about is ancient and unspoiled. The hill on one side rises like a sheltering wall of green and the lawn on the other slopes down to an enchanting lily pond.

Viele Jahrhunderte sind vergangen, seit Francesco Burlamacchi (1498–1548), ein berühmter Staatsmann und Gegenspieler der Medici, die arkadengeschmückte Villa erbaute. Zahlreiche persönliche Objekte und Kunstwerke zeugen von den verschiedenen Besitzern der Villa und deren Leben. Die ehrfurchtgebietenden höfischen Porträts, die heute das Speisezimmer beherrschen, stammen von einem holländischen Freund des französischen Kaisers Napoleon III. Der nächste Besitzer war der aus Lucca stammende Don Lorenzo Altieri, der das Mündel des Holländers, eine russische Prinzessin, heiratete. Heute ist die Schriftstellerin Francesca Duranti zurückgekehrt an den Ort ihrer Kindheit. Benannt ist das Anwesen Villa Rossi nach ihrem Vater Paolo Rossi, der es kurz vor Ausbruch des Zweiten Weltkriegs erwarb. Francescas ganzes Herz hängt an dem Haus und dessen immer noch unberührten Umgebung: dem Hügel, der sich wie ein grüner Schutzwall erhebt, und dem tiefer gelegenen Teich mit Lotosblüten.

Au premier étage, le salon décoré de fresques où se trouvait autrefois la bibliothèque. Un peintre local du 17e siècle l'a orné de fresques en trompe-l'œil; elles représentent des éléments d'architecture vus en perspective, des statues des Quatre Saisons et, au plafond, une allégorie de l'Aurore. Les grandes portes-fenêtres donnent sur une colline verdoyante.

The frescoed reception room on the first floor, which was originally used as a library. The frescoes, painted in the 17th century by a local artist, include "trompe-l'œil" architectural effects with perspectives, mock statues of the Four Seasons and an allegorical representation of Dawn on the ceiling. The French windows look out onto the rich vegetation of the hillside.

In dem mit Fresken geschmückten Salon im ersten Geschoß befand sich ursprünglich die Bibliothek. Die Fresken aus dem 17. Jahrhundert stammen von einem lokalen Künstler und beeindrucken durch perspektivische Scheinarchitekturen. Die Decke schmückt eine allegorische Darstellung der Aurora; die Wände zieren gemalte Statuen. Durch die hohen Fenstertüren leuchtet das Grün eines Hügels.

Page de gauche: *la salle à manger du rez-de-chaussée, d'où l'on aperçoit la bibliothèque. Au mur trône un portrait officiel de l'impératrice Eugénie de Montijo.*
Ci-dessus, à gauche: *l'arrière de la villa, avec la loggia, vu de la pente qui mène à l'étang.*
Ci-dessus, à droite: *l'étang et son petit pont; Francesca Duranti s'y promenait en barque lorsqu'elle était enfant.*

Facing page: *the dining room on the ground floor, looking through to the library. A formal portrait of the French Empress Eugenia de Montijo, wife of Napoleon III, hangs on the wall.*
Above left: *a rear view of the villa and portico from the slope leading down to the pond.*
Above right: *the bridge over the pond where the writer went boating as a child.*

Linke Seite: *Vom Speisezimmer im Erdgeschoß aus erhascht man einen Blick in die Bibliothek. An der Wand hängt ein offizielles Bildnis der französischen Kaiserin Eugénie, der Gemahlin Napoleons III.*
Oben links: *Blick auf die Rückseite der Villa mit der Loggia. Die Wiese führt zum Teich.*
Oben rechts: *die kleine Brücke über den Teich, auf dem Francesca als Kind Bootsfahrten unternahm.*

Igor Mitoraj

The picturesque village of Pietrasanta is situated high above the Tyrrhenian Sea in the province of Lucca. To this day, there are numerous traditional workshops there, where the white, finely veined marble from the nearby quarries of Carrara is artistically worked. It is where Igor Mitoraj, a sculptor of Polish origin, has chosen to set up his studio next to the rooms in which he lives. The house overlooks the road and the sculptor's work area backs onto the hillside, which was excavated to construct it. The internal spaces are in a classic Mediterranean style. "I was attracted to classical antiquity because I am extremely sensitive to the messages that ancient objects communicate," notes Mitoraj. It is above all in the garden that the artist's sculptures engage in a magically evocative dialogue with the remains of ancient statues, half-hidden among the oleanders and lemon trees.

Double page précédente, à droite: *dans le jardin, deux sculptures de l'artiste; le «Torse hivernal», en bronze, et le moulage en plâtre de «La Bouche», étude pour un monument destiné au siège de Coca-Cola, à Atlanta.*
Ci-dessus: *la maison et l'atelier.*
A droite: *la coursive avec des œuvres d'Igor Mitoraj: le buste «Tindare», la sculpture intitulée «Silence» de Janne Plenza, trois têtes en bronze «Deux I», la statue en marbre «Initiation» et le vase «Ile» (de gauche à droite).*
Page de droite: *le séjour, vu de la coursive. Près de l'escalier et de la porte, «Les Mains» et une tête en bronze intitulée «La Maison du sculpteur». Encastrée dans le sol, la fontaine «Gorgone», en marbre blanc. En haut, un petit temple en bois doré du 16e siècle.*

Previous pages, right: *works by Igor Mitoraj in the garden: a bronze entitled "Winter Torso" and "Mouth", a prototype cast of a monumental work for the Coca Cola headquarters in Atlanta.*
Above: *the house and the studio.*
Right: *a walkway with sculptures by Igor Mitoraj: the bust "Tindar", the sculpture "Silence" by Janne Plenza, three bronze heads "Two Is", the marble sculpture "Initiation" and the vase entitled "Island" (from left to right).*
Facing page: *the living room seen from the walkway. Near the stairs and the door are "Hands" and the bronze head "The Sculptor's House" by Mitoraj. The white marble fountain "Gorgon" is set in the floor. At the top of the photograph can be seen a 16th-century, gilt-wood shrine.*

Vorhergehende Doppelseite, rechts: *Im Garten befinden sich Igor Mitorajs Gipsabguß »Mund«, Modell eines monumentalen Werks für den vor dem Firmensitz von Coca-Cola in Atlanta, und die Bronze »Wintertorso«.*

Oben: *Wohnhaus und Atelier.*
Rechts: *In der Galerie stehen weitere Werke von Mitoraj: die Büste »Tyndareos«, die Skulptur »Stille« von Janne Plenza, die drei Bronzeköpfe »Zwei I«, die Marmorstatue »Initiation« und die Vase »Insel« (von links nach rechts).*
Rechte Seite: *Blick von der Galerie in den Wohnraum. Neben der Tür befinden sich »Die Hände« und der Bronzekopf »Das Haus des Bildhauers«. In den Fußboden eingelassen ist der weiße Marmorbrunnen »Gorgonenhaupt«. Auf der Galerie steht ein kleiner Rundtempel aus vergoldetem Holz aus dem 16. Jahrhundert.*

Tuscany Interiors   Igor Mitoraj

Double page précédente: L'atelier de l'artiste, à gauche, et sa demeure, se font face, séparés par un espace couvert d'un grand vélum blanc. Au premier plan, la «Tête de Nara», en marbre de Carrare, est l'œuvre d'Igor Mitoraj.

Page de gauche: L'atelier de l'artiste, creusé dans la roche, est éclairé par de grandes verrières. Des fragments de sculptures antiques, des moulages en plâtre et des œuvres en marbre de l'artiste sont disposés les uns à côté des autres dans un savant désordre.

Ci-dessus, à gauche: Devant une grande fenêtre de l'atelier, aux huisseries dessinées par Igor Mitoraj lui-même, on peut voir quelques moulages en plâtre de l'artiste, parmi lesquels, le «Torse ailé», au premier plan, «La Maison du sculpteur» (la tête de femme, au fond) et «Lumières de Nara» (la tête inclinée sans front, à gauche).

Ci-dessus, à droite: Toujours dans l'atelier, sa «Tête de Gorgone», au fond à gauche, et ses «Chasseurs de Gorgone», au premier plan à droite, apparaissent entre des moulages d'antiques.

Previous pages: Mitoraj's studio on the left and living quarters on the right face each other across a space covered by a huge white tarpaulin. In the foreground is "Nara's Head" in Carrara marble by Igor Mitoraj.

Facing page: Igor Mitoraj's studio is carved out of the living rock and lit naturally thanks to generously proportioned windows. Fragments of ancient sculptures, plaster casts and works in marble by Mitoraj rub shoulders in an attractively ordered chaos.

Above left: a series of plaster casts by Igor Mitoraj lined up at one of the large studio windows, whose fittings were designed by the artist himself. In the foreground is "Winged Torso", "The Sculptor's House"

(the woman's head in the background) and "Nara's Lights" (the inclined head without forehead on the left).

Above right: another view of the studio featuring ancient casts: "Gorgon's Head" in the background on the left, and "Gorgon Hunters", the two marble busts, in the right-hand foreground.

Vorhergehende Doppelseite: Durch die weiße Plane zwischen Wohnhaus und Atelier entsteht ein schattiger Platz. Im Vordergrund sieht man Igors »Nara-Kopf« aus Carrara-Marmor.

Linke Seite: Das Atelier mit den großen Fenstern ist direkt in den Felsen hineingebaut. Hier bilden Fragmente antiker Skulpturen, Gipsabgüsse und Marmorwerke von Mitoraj ein »geordnetes Chaos«.

Oben links: Vor einem Atelierfenster befinden sich einige Gipsabgüsse des Künstlers: im Vordergrund »Geflügelter Torso«, links daneben der geneigte Kopf ohne Stirn »Die Lichter von Nara«, dahinter der weibliche Kopf »Das Haus des Bildhauers«.

Oben rechts: Zwischen antiken Gipsabgüssen sieht man links die Arbeit »Gorgonenhaupt« und rechts die »Gorgonenjäger«.

Ci-dessus: La tablette de la cheminée accueille une série de petits objets et de sculptures. De gauche à droite: l'«Eponge bleue» d'Yves Klein, une tête antique, une œuvre de Niki de Saint-Phalle, une sculpture en fonte, «Torse avec C...» de Mitoraj, un dessin d'Enzo Cucchi, une «Corbeille de grenades» de Mitoraj.
Page de droite: un aspect du séjour qui communique avec la chambre à coucher. Les meubles de style Empire sont d'origine russe. Un grand tableau du peintre allemand Hermann Albert, «Le Constructeur», est appuyé au mur à côté de la porte.

Above: A small collection of sculptures and "objets d'art" graces the mantelpiece. From left to right: a "Blue Sponge" by Yves Klein, an ancient head, a sculpture by Niki de Saint-Phalle, a cast-iron sculpture entitled "Torso with C..." by Mitoraj, a drawing by Enzo Cucchi and a "Basket of Pomegranates" by Mitoraj.
Facing page: a view of the living room. The Empire furniture is from Russia. The large painting leaning against the wall near the door is "The Constructor" by the German painter Hermann Albert.

Oben: Auf dem Kaminsims befindet sich eine kleine Auswahl von Objekten und Skulpturen. Von links nach rechts: »Blauer Schwamm« von Yves Klein, eine antike Büste, eine Skulptur von Niki de Saint Phalle, Mitorajs Gußeisenskulptur »Torso mit C... «, eine Zeichnung von Enzo Cucchi und »Körbchen mit Granatäpfeln« von Mitoraj.
Rechte Seite: Ansicht des mit dem Schlafzimmer verbundenen Wohnraums. Die Empire-Möbel stammen aus Rußland. An der Wand neben der Tür lehnt das großformatige Gemälde »Der Erbauer« des deutschen Malers Hermann Albert.

La Villa de Notter se dresse au milieu d'un pré. Une haie l'isole du côté de la colline mais la façade principale jouit d'une vue imprenable sur la ville. L'édifice d'origine a été agrandi au 17e siècle; son aspect actuel, conforme à la typologie locale, présente une forme cubique, avec une loggia ornée d'une fresque représentant Oliver Cromwell, Alexandre le Grand et Jules César. Habitée sans interruption, la villa a toujours appartenu à la même famille et les souvenirs s'y sont accumulés. Des meubles et des objets d'époques diverses, consoles dorées florentines, dallages à la vénitienne, assiettes de la Compagnie des Indes témoignent de l'évolution du goût. Enfin, des hallebardes évoquent les condottieres dont descend la famille, et qui participèrent à la défense de Vienne contre les Turcs.

Villa de Notter

Villa de Notter stands amid lawns in a small village, commanding a fine view of Lucca from the windows of the main frontage. It has always been owned by the same family, descended from "condottieri"; their ancestors took part in many a military campaign, and fought the Turks before the gates of Vienna. Pride in that descent is manifest in the 19th-century frescoes in the loggia. They portray famous military leaders such as Alexander the Great, Julius Caesar and Oliver Cromwell. The furniture is a reminder that the house has been in continuous occupation down the centuries, and various features record the changes of taste: the gilt Florentine console tables, the valuable Venetian floors, the East India Company eggshell china, and the halberds that once belonged to soldier ancestors. Villa de Notter is a resplendent chronicle of bygone eras.

Mitten auf einer Wiese in einem kleinen Dorf steht die Villa de Notter. Von den Fenstern der Hauptfassade hat man einen herrlichen Blick auf Lucca. Die Villa ist seit jeher Familiensitz eines Geschlechts, das von »condottieri« abstammt. Als Heerführer waren die Vorfahren der de Notter an vielen kriegerischen Auseinandersetzungen beteiligt und kämpften auch vor Wien gegen die Türken. Vom Stolz auf die Herkunft zeugen die Fresken des 19. Jahrhunderts in der Loggia. Sie zeigen berühmte Heerführer wie Alexander den Großen, Julius Cäsar und Oliver Cromwell. Die Einrichtungsgegenstände belegen, daß das Haus über die Jahrhunderte hinweg ständig bewohnt war. Gleichzeitig läßt sich an der Ausstattung die Veränderung des Geschmacks im Laufe der Zeit ablesen: an den vergoldeten, florentinischen Konsoltischen, den wertvollen Fußböden im venezianischen Stil, dem dünnwandingen Porzellan der Ostindischen Kompanie und an den Hellebarden der Vorfahren – die Villa de Notter ist eine glanzvolle Chronik verschiedener Epochen.

Double page précédente: *vue de la villa. La loggia à trois arcades, typique de la region, fut amenagée au 17e siècle.*
Ci-dessus: *Le salon du rez-de-chaussée a conservé ses poutres apparentes. Le dallage à la vénitienne du 18e siècle est constitué de pouzzolane dans laquelle sont insérés des fragments de marbres polychromes; des tapis persans le couvrent. La console dorée et le miroir, d'origine florentine, datent de la seconde moitié du 19e siècle, de même que le lustre de bronze doré. Ces chaises lucquoises de style néoclassique sont surnommées localement «pattone».*

Previous pages: *a view of Villa de Notter with the three-lobed loggia characteristic of the village, which was created in the course of rebuilding in the 17th century.*
Above: *the ground-floor living room. The original ceiling beams have been conserved. The 18th-century terrazzo floor was laid on a base of pozzolan into which were set pieces of coloured marble. The carpets are Persian and the gilt console table and mirror were made in Florence in the latter half of the 19th century, as was the gilt bronze chandelier. The neoclassically-inspired chairs from Lucca are in the style known locally as "pattona".*

Vorhergehende Doppelseite: *die Villa mit der ortstypischen dreibogigen Loggia, die bei einem Umbau im 17. Jahrhundert entstand.*
Oben: *der Salon im Erdgeschoß. Der venezianische Fußboden aus dem 18. Jahrhundert besteht aus Puzzolan, einem porösen vulkanischen Tuffstein, mit farbiger Marmorauflage. Die vergoldete Konsole, der Spiegel und der Leuchter aus vergoldeter Bronze stammen aus dem Florenz der zweiten Hälfte des 19. Jahrhunderts. Die klassizistischen lucchesischen Stühle werden in der Region »pattone« genannt. An der Decke sind die Originalbalken erhalten, auf dem Fußboden liegen Perserteppiche.*

A droite: Une vitrine renferme une riche collection de porcelaines de la Compagnie des Indes.
Ci-dessous: La lumineuse salle à manger comporte des fresques du 18e siècle en trompe-l'œil, des sièges anglais et un lampadaire en bronze du 19e siècle.

Right: a display cabinet with a fine collection of East India Company porcelain.
Below: the well-lit dining room where English chairs stand underneath a 19th-century bronze chandelier surrounded by impressive "trompe-l'œil" frescoes dating from the 18th century.

Rechts: Die Vitrine beherbergt eine umfangreiche Sammlung von Porzellan der Ostindischen Kompanie.
Unten: In dem lichtdurchfluteten Speisezimmer beeindrucken gemalte Scheinarchitekturen aus dem 18. Jahrhundert. Auch die Einrichtung ist antik: die englischen Sitzmöbel und der Bronzeleuchter stammen aus dem 19. Jahrhundert.

Villa La Maolina

Villa La Maolina lies in a stunning location at the foot of the Apuan Alps amid woods, vineyards and olive groves. It is a "fattoria", a working agricultural estate, as well as a country residence, with several holdings and tenant farmers' houses, whose olive oil and wine have contributed to its fame. The owners spend as much time as possible on the estate, alternating its uncomplicated lifestyle with the faster pace of nearby Lucca. A balustraded double flight of steps takes the visitor up to a large glass-fronted door leading straight into the main reception room, where an 18th-century wood-topped billiard table is the undisputed focus of attention. Guests are entertained both in summer and in winter, when the rooms are heated by stoves or fireplaces and the smell of woodsmoke mingles with that of meat roasting in the huge kitchen. Measuring over sixty square metres, it is the heart of life at the villa.

Double page précédente, à gauche: *la Villa La Maolina; la salle du billard.*
Double page précédente, à droite: *des verres anciens.*
Ci-dessus: *la salle de bal au magnifique pavement de marbre marqueté. Les fresques et les décorations murales datent de la fin du 18e siècle, ainsi que les deux longs divans adossés au mur et le guéridon placé entre eux. Le lustre vient de Murano.*

Previous pages, left: *Villa La Maolina; the billiard room.*
Previous pages, right: *antique glasses.*
Above: *The ballroom floor is inlaid marble floor. The frescoes and decorations on the walls date back to the end of the 18th century, as do the two long sofas standing against the wall and the table that separates them. The chandelier is in Murano glass.*

Vorhergehende Doppelseite, links: *die Villa La Maolina; das Billardzimmer.*
Vorhergehende Doppelseite, rechts: *alte Gläser.*
Oben: *der prunkvolle Ballsaal, dessen Fußboden reich mit Marmoreinlegearbeiten verziert ist. Die Fresken und Wanddekorationen stammen aus dem ausgehenden 18. Jahrhundert, ebenso wie die beiden Sofas an der Wand und der dazwischen stehende kleine Tisch. Der Leuchter ist aus Muranoglas.*

*A **droite:*** *un salon au mobilier Empire, style qui prédomine dans la Villa La Maolina.*
Ci-dessous: *un autre salon avec sa cheminée; le lampadaire de cristal et les tableaux accrochés au mur datent de la fin du 18e siècle, alors que les divans et les fauteuils sont modernes; au sol, des tapis persans.*

Right: *a drawing room with Empire furniture; the predominant style at Villa La Maolina.*
Below: *another reception room with fireplace and a late 18th-century glass chandelier. The paintings on the walls also date from the same period but the sofas and armchairs are modern. The carpets are Persian.*

Rechts: *ein Salon mit Empire-Möbeln. Die meisten Räume sind in diesem Stil eingerichtet.*
Unten: *ein weiterer Salon mit Kamin. Der Kristalleuchter und die Gemälde stammen aus dem ausgehenden 18. Jahrhundert. Persische Teppiche sowie moderne Sofas und Sessel vervollständigen die Einrichtung.*

Ci-dessus: le lit à baldaquin; la structure date du 19e siècle et est re-vêtue de tissus modernes choisis avec soin pour s'harmoniser avec le style d'origine. Les propriétaires actuels de la villa ont trouvé ce lit sur place.
Page de droite: la coiffeuse date du 19e siècle et elle est recouverte de tissus qui, avec les rideaux drapés, restituent l'esprit romantique de l'époque. Au fond, une commode à miroir du 19e siècle.

Above: a four-poster bed whose structure dates from the 19th century. The fabrics have been selected with great care to reflect the style of the period. The bed was found in the villa by the present owners.
Facing page: The 19th-century dressing table has been covered with modern fabrics to capture the romantic spirit of the age that inspired its design, which is also reflected in the luxurious sweep of the cur-tains. In the background is a chest of drawers on which stands a 19th-century mirror.

Oben: Dieses Himmelbett fanden die derzeitigen Besitzer im Schlaf-zimmer vor. Das Originalgestell aus dem 19. Jahrhundert ist mit dem Stil jener Epoche entsprechend ausgewählten Stoffen sorgfältig be-spannt.
Rechte Seite: In diesem Schlafzimmer fühlt man sich in die Roman-tik zurückversetzt. Die Stoffe des Toilettentischs wurden zum Stil pas-send ausgewählt. Die Spiegelkommode im Hintergrund stammt aus dem 19. Jahrhundert.

Double page précédente: la cuisine du 18e siècle, avec sa table en bois massif, ses chaises de paille rustiques, ses meubles et ses étagères pour poser les ustensiles. A l'origine, la villa se trouvait au centre d'une exploitation qui produisait du vin et employait un grand nombre de personnes. La cuisine constituait le cœur de ce microcosme et se devait d'être avant tout vaste et fonctionnelle. Elle est restée telle quelle, même si de nombreux ustensiles ne servent plus. Le lustre en fer forgé et les poutres du plafond sont également d'origine.
Page de gauche: Dans la cuisine, sur les étagères, on peut voir une belle collection d'ustensiles et de récipients anciens de grandes dimensions, surtout en cuivre. Aujourd'hui rarement utilisés, ils servaient autrefois durant les vendanges, car un grand nombre de travailleurs se retrouvaient alors dans la villa.
Ci-dessus, à gauche: deux énormes bidons en cuivre qui devaient servir quand il y avait beaucoup de monde.
Ci-dessus, à droite: Les vieux robinets, du 18e siècle comme tout le reste, ont été amoureusement conservés.

Previous pages: a view of the original 18th-century kitchen, its imposing wooden table, the straw-bottomed chairs and the cupboards and shelves for storing kitchen utensils. The villa was built as the focal point of a winemaking estate that gave employment to a considerable number of agricultural workers. At the heart of this busy concern was the kitchen, which had to be large and functional. It has been left as it was in its heyday, although much of the kitchen equipment is no longer used. Even the wrought-iron chandelier and the beamed ceiling are original.
Facing page: The kitchen shelves feature a display of objects from the past. Most are bulky copper utensils that are rarely used nowadays.

At one time they were called into service during the grape harvest when many casual workers came to the villa to help with the vintage.
Above left: two immense copper cans that were used on occasions when large numbers of seasonal workers were employed on the estate.
Above right: the original taps, which date from the 18th century like everything else that has been so lovingly conserved in the kitchen.

Vorhergehende Doppelseite: die Originalküche aus dem 18. Jahrhundert mit dem wuchtigen Holztisch, rustikalen Stühlen mit Strohgeflecht und verschiedenen Küchengerätschaften. Früher war die Küche das Herz des ehemaligen Weinguts, auf dem zahlreiche Menschen beschäftigt waren. Deshalb mußte sie vor allem geräumig und praktisch sein. Verändert hat sich in der Küche kaum etwas, weder die schmiedeeisernen Leuchter noch die Deckenbalken – lediglich einige Utensilien sind heute nicht mehr in Gebrauch.
Linke Seite: eine wunderschöne Sammlung von alten Küchengeräten in den Regalen. Die meisten Gegenstände bestehen aus Kupfer und sind auffallend groß, denn in ihnen wurde während der Weinlese das Essen für die vielen Erntehelfer zubereitet.
Oben links: Während der Erntezeit wurden in der Küche große Kupferkannen verwendet.
Oben rechts: Wie alle anderen Gegenstände in der Küche werden auch die Wasserhähne liebevoll gepflegt.

A Forte dei Marmi, station de villégiature renommée et élégante, les villas du quartier baptisé «Roma Imperiale» ont été construites dans les années trente pour y passer des vacances tranquilles, à l'écart du front de mer trop bruyant. L'architecte florentin Sergio Castelfranco a conçu la Villa Antonietta en 1936–1937 pour la famille des propriétaires actuels. Au fil des années, la villa avait quelque peu perdu de son éclat. Gabriella Zini Pazzi et son mari, l'avocat Alessandro Pazzi, qui y passent l'été et y sont très attachés, l'ont donc restaurée en s'efforçant de préserver le plus fidèlement possible son esprit particulier. Ils ont conservé l'ameublement de l'époque, et pour remplacer les éléments disparus, ils ont acheté des meubles, des objets et des œuvres d'art des années trente chez des antiquaires.

Villa Antonietta

This is how the privileged few used to enjoy their holidays at the elegant seaside resort of Forte dei Marmi, hidden safely away from the hubbub of the seafront, in villas built during the Thirties in the Roma Imperiale district. The owners of Villa Antonietta, Signora Gabriella Zini Pazzi and her lawyer husband Alessandro Pazzi, are members of the family that commissioned the Florentine architect Sergio Castelfranco to design the property in 1936–37. Over the years, Villa Antonietta had begun to lose some of its vitality and freshness, so the couple, who come here to spend the summer and have a keen sense of the villa's place in local tradition, have restored it while conserving its original character. Even some of the original furnishings have been restored and the gaps filled by furniture, ornaments and works of art from the same period that the owners have purchased from antiquarians.

Wer in das elegante Seebad Forte dei Marmi in die Sommerfrische fährt, bevorzugt das Wohnen im noblen Villenviertel Roma Imperiale. Abseits der lauten Strandpromenade stehen dort zwischen schattigen Alleen Villen der dreißiger Jahre. Dort liegt auch die hübsche Villa Antonietta, in die sich Gabriella Zini Pazzi und ihr Mann, der Rechtsanwalt Alessandro Pazzi, regelmäßig in den heißen Sommermonaten zurückziehen. Sie hängen sehr an der Villa, die 1936–37 von dem florentinischen Architekten Sergio Castelfranco für ihre Familie erbaut wurde, und gingen bei der Restaurierung mit viel Fingerspitzengefühl vor. Tatsächlich gelang es ihnen auch, die ursprüngliche Innenausstattung teilweise zu rekonstruieren und Originalstücke aus der Entstehungszeit der Villa in Antiquitätengeschäften aufzustöbern. In der eleganten Villa Antonietta erwacht der klare Geist der dreißiger Jahre zu neuem Leben.

Double page précédente, à gauche: *La silhouette de la villa résulte du contraste de volumes arrondis et cubiques; l'escalier externe avec sa rambarde incurvée; jeu d'ombre et de lumière dans l'escalier du vestibule.*

Double page précédente, à droite: *La salle à manger au mobilier d'origine est contiguë à l'escalier.*

Page de gauche: *détail de la chambre des maîtres de maison avec une coiffeuse art déco.*

Ci-dessus: *Le séjour est meublé d'objets trouvés chez des antiquaires. A gauche, on voit notamment une console signée Guglielmo Ulrich.*

Previous pages, left: *Villa Antonietta's profile juxtaposes contrasting round and square volumes; the external stairs and curved parapet; play of light and shadow in the stairwell of the entrance hall.*

Previous pages, right: *The dining room with the original furniture is next to the staircase.*

Facing page: *a detail of the master bedroom with a beautiful Art Deco dressing table.*

Above: *The living-room furniture is contemporary with the villa, including on the left a Guglielmo Ulrich console.*

Vorhergehende Doppelseite, links: *Charakteristisch für das Gebäude ist der Gegensatz zwischen runden und quadratischen Formen; die Außentreppe mit einem geschwungenen Geländer; Spiel von Licht und Schatten im Treppenhaus.*

Vorhergehende Doppelseite, rechts: *Neben der Treppe liegt das mit Möbeln aus den dreißiger Jahren ausgestattete Speisezimmer.*

Linke Seite: *Teilansicht des Schlafzimmers des Ehepaars mit einem besonders schönen Art-Deco-Schminktisch.*

Oben: *Die Einrichtungsgegenstände des Wohnzimmers stammen aus Antiquitätengeschäften. Links eine Anrichte von Guglielmo Ulrich.*

Ci-dessus: La cuisine bleue, conçue par Pietro Pescarolo, reprend la typologie de celle qui existait à l'origine.
Page de droite: Des meubles des années trente achetés chez des antiquaires ornent une pièce d'angle. Le lampadaire aux petits oiseaux est l'une des dernières créations de la verrerie Cappellin qui ferma vers la fin des années trente.

Above: The blue kitchen, by Pietro Pescarolo, follows the original design.
Facing page: Furniture dating from the Thirties, when the villa was built, has been acquired for this corner room. The bird-cage chandelier was one of the last pieces of ornamental ironworks made by the glassworks Cappellin, which closed at the end of the Thirties.

Oben: Pietro Pescarolo entwarf die blaue Küche im Stil der dreißiger Jahre.
Rechte Seite: Ein Eckzimmer wurde mit Möbelstücken aus der Entstehungszeit der Villa eingerichtet. Die Lampe mit den Vögelchen ist eines der letzten Produkte der venezianischen Glasbläserei Cappellin, die Ende der dreißiger Jahre geschlossen wurde.

*Dynamiques et pleins de fantaisie, Claudio Brocchini et son épouse
ont su créer une demeure extraordinaire dont les couleurs vives se
voient de loin. Ils ont transformé une ancienne «casa colonica», une
ferme du 19e siècle, proche de Viareggio, en un étonnant patchwork
d'objets, de couleurs et d'impressions de voyage. Fils d'un antiquaire,
Claudio a toujours su déceler l'esprit poétique des choses, leur beauté
secrète, les affinités fascinantes et mystérieuses qu'elles suggèrent.
«Chaque objet représente pour moi un souvenir, une circonstance
particulière, une personne rencontrée; ils viennent d'endroits extrêmement divers, bien que l'on dénote une attirance plus particulière pour
l'Amérique du Nord et l'Afrique». Ici, les extravagances apparentes,
les dissonances ironiques et les rapprochements incongrus obéissent
en fait à un profond sens de l'harmonie.*

Claudio Brocchini

The energy and imagination of Claudio Brocchini and his wife have
created this extraordinary house. It is a very personal treasure trove
of assorted objects, colours and souvenirs from their travels. They
are all gathered together under the roof of a former 19th-century
"casa colonica", a tenant farmer's house, near Viareggio, which is
easily identified thanks to its vivid exterior. Brocchini, the son of an
antique expert, was brought up to recognize the poetic soul that is
hidden inside objects, their secret beauty and their relationship
with the mysterious world of mental connotations. "Each object,"
he will tell you, "for me is a memory, an experience or someone I
have known in some far corner of the world, although I have a particular affection for North America and Africa". The apparent ex-
travagance, the tongue-in-cheek contrasts and the unexpected
combinations are reconciled by a profound sense of harmony.

*Die überschäumende Lebensfreude und Fantasie von Claudio Bro-
cchini und seiner Ehefrau ließen ein außergewöhnliches Heim ent-
stehen. Schon von weitem leuchtet dem Besucher die farbenprächtige
»casa colonica« entgegen, ein ehemaliges Pächterhaus aus dem 19.
Jahrhundert. Hier, in der Nähe von Viareggio, haben die Brocchinis
ihren ganz privaten Basar eingerichtet – ein Sammelsurium von zahllosen Reiseerinnerungen und ungewöhnlichen Objekten in den lebhaf-
testen Farben. Als Sohn eines Antiquitätenhändlers lernte Claudio
Brocchini bereits als Kind, hinter die Dinge zu schauen, ihre poetische
Seele und verborgene Schönheit zu entdecken. »Jeder Gegenstand«,
erzählt er begeistert, »erinnert mich an besondere Erlebnisse oder
Menschen, denen ich in einem entlegenen Winkel der Welt begegnet
bin. Nordamerika und Afrika liebe ich ganz besonders.« Das schein-
bar Exzentrische, die ironischen Brechungen und die ungewöhnlichen
Zusammenstellungen bezeugen einen völlig eigenständigen Sinn für
Harmonie.*

Page précédente: un détail du séjour; sur la table en mosaïque de verre coloré réalisée par l'artisan Mauro Marcucci, on note un ensemble américain des années quarante et un plateau de verre opalin italien de la même époque. L'armoire a été dessinée par une jeune créatrice nommée Elise, au Nouveau-Mexique, d'où vient aussi le divan. Sur la table basse indienne au plateau de cuivre, on remarque un cierge turc et, plus haut sur le mur, un entonnoir à essence américain.

Ci-dessus: La cuisine est meublée d'une table «Taos», d'une chaise américaine, d'une chaise française de 1934 en métal zingué et d'une chaise en cerisier classique du Vermont; à droite, un panneau publicitaire anglais.

Page de droite, dans le sens des aiguilles d'une montre: dans une chambre d'enfant, une moto en bois d'un manège anglais du début du siècle et un casque de pompier; un petit fauteuil américain, une tablette avec son miroir des années cinquante, d'origine française, et une lampe «Parentesi» créée par Achille Castiglioni; dans la cuisine, au-dessus de la table réalisée par Mauro Marcucci et de la chaise Shaker de Jan Ingersoll, sont accrochées deux enseignes publicitaires à côté d'un tableau de Giovanni Raffaelli – un brocanteur artiste surnommé «Le Tatoué»; derrière la roue d'une bicyclette de course américaine, on aperçoit une forme à gants italienne.

Previous pages: detail of the living room. On the glass mosaic table, by the craftsman Mauro Marcucci, is an American table set and an Italian opaline glass tray, both made in the Forties. The cupboard was made by a young designer called Elise, in New Mexico. The sofa is also from New Mexico. A Turkish candle stands on the Indian table with its bronze top. Hanging higher up on the wall is an American petrol funnel.

Above: The kitchen features a "Taos" table, a chair from America, a 1934 French galvanized metal chair and a classic Vermont chair in cherrywood. On the right is a British advertising sign.

Facing page, clockwise from top left: a wooden motorcycle from an early 20th-century fairground ride and a fireman's helmet in one of the children's bedrooms; an American aluminium chair, a French shelf and mirror from the Fifties and a "Parentesi" lamp by Achille Castiglioni; a Shaker chair by Jan Ingersoll at a table by Mauro Marcucci in the kitchen. On the wall next to the painting by Giovanni Raffaelli, a second-hand dealer and artist known as the "Tattooed Man", hang two advertising signs.

Vorhergehende Seite: Teilansicht des Wohnraums. Auf dem Tisch des Kunsthandwerkers Mauro Marcucci – die Platte schmückt ein Mosaik aus farbigen Glassteinchen – stehen ein amerikanisches Trinkset und ein italienisches Tablett aus Opalglas. Beides wurde in den vierziger Jahren gefertigt. Der Schrank ist ein Entwurf von Elise aus New Mexico, von woher auch das Sofa stammt. Auf dem niedrigen indischen Tischchen mit Messingplatte befindet sich eine Wachskerze aus der Türkei. Darüber hängt ein amerikanischer Trichter zum Einfüllen von Benzin.

Oben: Zur Kücheneinrichtung gehören der Tisch »Taos«, ein amerikanischer Stuhl, ein französischer Stuhl aus verzinktem Metall von 1934 und ein klassischer Kirschbaumstuhl aus Vermont. Rechts im Bild ein englisches Werbeplakat.

Rechte Seite, im Uhrzeigersinn von links oben: Das Holzmotorrad unter dem Feuerwehrhelm im Kinderzimmer drehte sich zu Beginn des Jahrhunderts auf einem Karussell in England; ein amerikanischer Armlehnstuhl aus Aluminium, die Leuchte »Parentesi« von Achille Castiglioni und ein französisches Wandbord mit Spiegel aus den fünfziger Jahren; in der Küche hängen zwei Werbeplakate und ein Gemälde des Künstlers und Altwarenhändlers Giovanni Raffaelli, genannt »Der Tätowierte«, über einem Tisch von Mauro Marcucci und einem Shaker-Stuhl von Jan Ingersoll; hinter den Speichen eines amerikanischen Rennrads ist eine italienische Handschuhform zu erkennen.

Double page précédente: le séjour. Sur la peau de zèbre, un petit fauteuil américain des années quarante ayant appartenu à un capitaine de l'armée des Etats-Unis. Le divan vient du Nouveau-Mexique, comme l'armoire d'Elise, au fond. Un masque africain orne le mur de gauche, et le siège du centre, au premier plan, est un trône amérindien fabriqué à partir de branchages et de peau de porc. La lampe de table en mosaïque vient de New York. Dans la niche, à droite, se trouvent une cruche américaine, un buste africain en ébène et un portrait anonyme.

Ci-dessous: la pièce de passage avec l'escalier qui mène aux chambres à coucher, à l'étage supérieur. Le petit meuble sur lequel est posé un cactus est un piédestal de cirque, probablement destiné aux fauves; à côté, une armoire autrichienne du début du 19e siècle et un miroir de Mauro Marcucci.

Previous pages: the living room. On the zebra skin stands a classic American chair from the Forties. It belonged to a captain in the United States Army. The sofa is from New Mexico, which is also where the cupboard by Elise in the far right-hand corner was made. An African mask hangs on the left-hand wall and the chair in the middle of the foreground is designed after a Native American throne made of branches and pigskin. The mosaic table lamp is from New York. In the recess on the right is an American jug, an early 20th-century ebony bust from Africa and an anonymous portrait.

Below: the connecting room with different objects. The vase of cactus is standing on what used to be a pedestal in a circus, probably used for wild animals. Next to it is an early 19th-century Austrian cupboard and a mirror by Mauro Marcucci.

Vorhergehende Doppelseite: Im Wohnraum steht auf einem Zebrafell ein klassischer amerikanischer Armlehnstuhl aus den vierziger Jahren, der einem Hauptmann der amerikanischen Armee gehörte. Das Sofa stammt wieder aus New Mexico; den Schrank im Hintergrund entwarf Elise. Links hängt eine afrikanische Maske an der Wand. Das Sitzmöbel im Vordergrund, aus Ästen und Schweinsleder gefertigt, ist einem indianischen Häuptlingsthron nachempfunden. Die Mosaiktischleuchte stammt aus New York. In der Nische rechts befinden sich eine amerikanische Vase, eine afrikanische Ebenholzbüste aus dem frühen 20. Jahrhundert und das Porträt eines Unbekannten.

Unten: Im Durchgangszimmer, von dem eine Treppe zu den Schlafzimmern im Obergeschoß führt, sind die unterschiedlichsten Objekte versammelt. Der Kaktus steht auf einem Zirkus-Piedestal, auf dem einst Löwen und Tiger saßen. Über einem österreichischen Schrank aus dem frühen 19. Jahrhundert hängt ein Spiegel von Mauro Marcucci.

La chambre d'enfant aux couleurs vives. L'armoire a été réalisée par Elise, au Nouveau-Mexique, comme le lit. Une plaque d'immatriculation américaine surmonte le bureau avec la lampe «Luxo». A droite, une moto en bois provenant d'un manège anglais.

One of the children's rooms is decorated in bright colours. The wardrobe was made by Elise in New Mexico, as was the bed. An American number plate hangs over the table with the "Luxo" lamp. On the right is a wooden motorcycle from a British fairground ride.

Das Kinderzimmer ist mit viel Fantasie und Gespür für lebhafte Farben eingerichtet. Den Schrank entwarf Elise. Auch das Bett stammt aus New Mexico. Über dem Arbeitstisch mit der Leuchte »Luxo« hängt ein amerikanisches Highway-Schild.

La salle de bains est entièrement revêtue d'une mosaïque de petits
carreaux. Tous les accessoires sont en métal: les étagères industrielles
américaines, la petite poubelle, le tabouret français de 1934 et la
lampe réalisée par le maître de maison lui-même.

The bathroom is tiled throughout with mosaic tessera tiles. The furnishings, all in metal, include American industrial shelving, a waste-
paper basket, a 1934 French tabouret stool and a lamp that was put
together by the owner of the house.

Sämtliche Einrichtungsgegenstände in dem mit Mosaikkacheln ge-
fliesten Bad sind aus Metall: das amerikanische Industrieregal, der
Abfalleimer, der französische Hocker von 1934 und die vom Hausherrn selbst entworfene Leuchte.

Tuscany Interiors   Claudio Brocchini

Dans la chambre à coucher, à la tête de lit «british sunrise» provenant de Santa Fé, on remarque au premier plan, de gauche à droite, une chaise suédoise anonyme, un vide-poches suédois des années cinquante en formica et en cuivre avec des récipients en mélamine, et un petit fauteuil en métal français de 1934.

The bed in the main bedroom features a "British Sunrise" bedhead from Santa Fé. In the foreground, from left to right, are a Swedish chair, a Formica-and-bronze Fifties Swedish table with melamine containers and a 1934 French metal armchair.

Das Bett aus Santa Fé im Schlafzimmer besitzt ein »British Sunrise«-Kopfteil. Rechts vor dem Bett steht ein französischer Metallstuhl aus dem Jahr 1934, links daneben befinden sich ein Stuhl und ein Beistelltisch schwedischer Produktion. Das Tischchen aus den fünfziger Jahren besteht aus Kunststoff und Messing mit Behältern aus Melamin.

Edifiée en 1766 à Avenza, près de Carrare, pour les comtes Orsolini, la Villa Monticello n'était à l'origine qu'une modeste résidence campagnarde. Mais à la fin du 19e siècle, elle fut achetée par une famille française, les Dervillé, qui décida de la transformer pour la rendre plus fastueuse. On fit ériger le grand escalier monumental bordé de statues et de fragments de sculptures antiques, ajouter des loggias sur trois côtés, des vases de marbre aux angles du toit et un fronton, de marbre également. Enfin, on construisit sur l'arrière un magnifique escalier de marbre blanc permettant d'accéder directement au salon du premier étage. La Villa Monticello appartient aujourd'hui à Madame Marzia Vanelli Dazzi, qui occupe avec son mari et ses enfants aussi bien le «piano nobile» à l'aspect solennel que le rez-de-chaussée plus intime. La mer est toute proche et l'été, la villa accueille toujours de nombreux amis.

Villa Monticello

When it was built in 1766 by the counts of Orsolini at Avenza, near Carrara, Villa Monticello was just a small country retreat. And so it remained until it was acquired in the late 19th century by the French Dervillé family, who enlarged and embellished it in exquisite taste. They added grand flights of steps at the front and back, and built loggias on three sides. Statues and fragments of ancient sculptures adorned the frontage while marble vases and a marble gable were placed on the roof. Today Villa Monticello is owned by Marzia Vanelli Dazzi, who lives there with her husband and children, occupying both the magnificently sumptuous "piano nobile" and the more modestly proportioned accommodation on the ground floor. In summer, the villa's location near the coast ensures that the family are never short of visiting friends to entertain.

Die Villa Monticello liegt in Avenza nahe Carrara und wurde im Jahre 1766 als bescheidenes Landhaus für die Grafen Orsolini errichtet. Die Familie Dervillé aus Frankreich erweiterte es Ende des 19. Jahrhunderts zu einer prachtvollen Villa mit Loggien an drei Seiten des Gebäudes. Aus dieser Zeit stammen auch die mit Statuen und Fragmenten antiker Statuen geschmückte Freitreppe und das marmorne Tympanon. An der rückwärtigen Fassade schließlich führt eine beeindruckende Treppe aus weißem Marmor direkt hinauf in den Salon. Heute bewohnt Marzia Vanelli Dazzi gemeinsam mit ihrem Mann und ihren Kindern die elegante Villa. Während des Sommers sind hier zahlreiche Freunde zu Gast, zumal das Meer ganz in der Nähe liegt.

Double page précédente: La loggia du premier étage, à l'arrière de la villa, offre le beau panorama des Alpes apuanes et des carrières de marbre. Les balustrades, les colonnes et le dallage à carreaux gris et blancs sont en marbre.

Ci-dessus: L'espace du séjour, au rez-de-chaussée, est rythmé par les colonnes de marbre blanc qui soutiennent les voûtes décorées du plafond. La petite table sur laquelle est posée un petit temple et les deux piédestaux surmontés de bustes en terre cuite qui flanquent la porte datent du 18e siècle et sont d'origine française, alors que le tapis vient de Chine.

A droite: une loggia au rez-de-chaussée, fermée par une grille basse de fer forgé. La paroi interne est décorée d'un bandeau de carreaux de faïence polychromes.

Previous pages: view from the first-floor loggia at the rear of the house looking out over the Apuan Alps and marble quarries. The balustrade, columns and grey-and-white chequered floor are all in marble.

Above: The ground-floor living area is divided up harmoniously by the white marble columns that support the vaulted ceiling. The table with the shrine and the pair of pedestal tables supporting the two terracotta busts on either side of the door are French and date from the 18th century. The carpet is Chinese.

Right: one of the loggias on the ground floor, closed off by a wrought-iron gate. The internal wall is decorated with a colourful fascia of tiles.

Vorhergehende Doppelseite: Von der rückwärtigen Loggia im ersten Stock blickt man auf die Apuanischen Alpen und die Marmorbrüche von Carrara. Die Brüstung, die Säulen und der weißgrau gewürfelte Boden sind aus Marmor.

Oben: Der Wohnraum im Erdgeschoß mit den prachtvoll dekorierten Deckengewölben wird durch marmorne Säulen unterteilt. Auf dem chinesischen Teppich steht ein Tisch mit einem Miniaturtempel. Er stammt ebenso wie die beiden Piedestale mit den Terrakottabüsten aus dem Frankreich des 18. Jahrhunderts.

Rechts: Eine Loggia im Erdgeschoß wird von einem kleinen schmiedeeisernen Tor abgeschlossen. Farbige Kacheln zieren die Innenwand der Loggia.

*A **droite:** Le blason en mosaïque de marbre, au centre du pavement du salon du premier étage, que l'on voit ici d'en haut, est celui de la famille Orsolini qui a édifié le noyau original de la villa.*
Ci-dessous: le salon du premier étage, sur lequel donnent toutes les chambres. Les parois sont ornées de fresques représentant des scènes mythologiques, entourées de faux cadres peints. Au-dessus de chaque porte à l'encadrement de marbre, on peut voir des médaillons de marbre du 18e siècle. Les chaises dorées qui jouxtent les deux consoles baroques sont de classiques «pattone» lucquoises. La table ronde est de style Empire et le lustre restauré d'origine française date du 18e siècle.

Right: a bird's-eye view of the marble mosaic crest on the floor of the reception room on the "piano nobile". The emblem is that of the Orsolini family, who rebuilt the original core of the villa.
Below: the first-floor reception room from which all the bedrooms lead off. The walls are decorated with frescoes of mythological subjects enclosed in fake painted frames. The marble architraves of the doors are surmounted by 18th-century medallions, also in marble. The two console tables are Baroque while the two gilt chairs are in the characteristic Luccan "pattona" style. The round table is Empire and the chandelier, which has been restored, is an 18th-century piece from France.

Rechts: Das Wappen der Orsolini, die den Kernbau der Villa errichteten, schmückt als Marmormosaik den Fußboden des Salons im ersten Geschoß.
Unten: Um den Salon im ersten Geschoß sind sämtliche Schlafzimmer angeordnet. Die Wände schmücken mythologische Szenen in gemalten Rahmen. Über den Türen mit Marmorpfosten prunken große Marmormedaillons aus dem 18. Jahrhundert. Unter dem restaurierten französischen Lüster aus demselben Jahrhundert steht ein Empiretisch. Im Hintergrund sind barocke Konsoltische und typisch lucchesische »pattona«-Stühle zu sehen.

Ci-dessus: la salle à manger pavée de marbre, aux grandes baies ou-
vrant sur le jardin et aux voûtes ornées de fresques. A côté des vases
chinois, un buste baroque. Sur la table mise, on voit des assiettes du
18e siècle. Les chaises qui l'entourent sont d'origine anglaise et le
buffet du 18e siècle à incrustations d'ébène, au fond, provient de
Ferrare.
Page de droite: une chambre à coucher aux parois et au plafond or-
nés de fresques élégantes. Les meubles et le buste en terre cuite, dans
l'angle, sont d'origine française.

Above: The glass doors in the marble-floored dining room open onto
the garden, the vaults are frescoed and a Baroque bust stands alongside vases from China. The chairs around the table, which is set with
18th-century porcelain, are English while the marquetry cabinet on
the far wall was made in Ferrara in the 18th century.
Facing page: a bedroom with elegantly frescoed walls and ceiling.
The furniture and the terracotta bust in the corner come from France.

Oben: Das Eßzimmer mit seinem wunderschönen Marmorfußboden
und den freskierten Stichkappen ist ein wahres Schmuckstück. Durch
große Flügelfenster blickt man in den Garten. Um den mit einem
Service aus dem 18. Jahrhundert gedeckten Tisch sind englische
Stühle gruppiert. Neben der Barockbüste stehen chinesische Vasen.
Der Schrank aus dem 18. Jahrhundert mit Ebenholzintarsien stammt
aus Ferrara.
Rechte Seite: ein Schlafzimmer mit eleganten Fresken. Die Möbel
und die Terrakottabüste in der Ecke stammen aus Frankreich.

Acknowledgements / Remerciements / Danksagung

First of all I would like to dedicate this book to the memory of
Walter Albini, my closest friend, who died a few years ago and
whom I miss very much. I would also like to thank the owners of
all the castles, palazzi, villas, apartments and country houses
who have been kind enough to grant permission for publication,
enduring the unavoidable intrusions of myself and our photographers and replying to my frequent enquiries. In particular,
I would like to express my thanks to Marquis Piero and Marchioness Francesca Antinori, Eva-Maria Arnds von Berlepsch, Luigi
Baldacci, Horst Bauer and Jürgen Weiss, Maria Gloria Conti
Bicocchi, Guglielmo Bonacchi, Carla Bonelli, Claudio Brocchini,
Massimo and Gabriella Ioli Carmassi, Piero Castellini, Sandro
Chia and Marella Caracciolo, Marzia Vanelli Dazzi, Joyce Dittemore, Francesca Duranti, Countess Cesarina Pannocchieschi
d'Elci, Wanda Ferragamo, Rita Foschi, Isanna Generali, Igor
Mitoraj, Pier Luigi de Notter, Gianni Nunziante, Alessandro and
Gabriella Zini Pazzi, Giovanni Pratesi, Marchioness Cristina
Pucci, Alfio Rapisardi, Baron Francesco Ricasoli, Francesco Ron-
cioni, Matthew and Maro Spender. And of course all those who
prefer to remain anonymous. My very special thanks go to
photographers Mario Ciampi and Simon Upton; and thanks are
also due to photographers Giorgio Baroni, Gianni Basso, Oliver
Benn, Santi Caleca, Anita Calero, Enrico Conti, Giovanna Dal
Magro, Giancarlo Gardin, Gianni Berengo Gardin, Oberto Gili,
Reto Guntli, Massimo Listri, Simon McBride, Bärbel Miebach,
Massimo Pacifico and Matteo Piazza, as well as to the following
photographic agencies: The Condé Nast Publications Inc., Frank
Parvis, Franca Speranza, Vega MG and Elizabeth Whiting & Asso-
ciates. I would also like to thank "Casa Vogue", "Casa Vogue
Antiques", "AD Italia", "AD Germania", "Abitare", "Domus",
"Casaviva", "La Mia Casa", "Case & Country", "Area", "House and
Garden", "The Sunday Telegraph Magazine", "World of Interiors",
"Period Living", "Ambiente" and "Madame", where some of the
features were first published, together with the journalists and
writers who wrote the relevant articles: Paolo Bartolini, Eugenio
Busmanti, Giuseppe Chigiotti, Francesco Dal Co, Nicoletta Don,
Luigi Emanuele, Enzo Fabiani, Massimo Griffi, Bernd Herborn,
Horst Heynemann, Clelia Littelton, Stefania Kuster, Charles
MacLean, Veit Mölter, Verena Niemeyer, Marco Romanelli, Miro
Silvera, Rodolfo Tommasi and Roberto Valeriani. Thanks also go
to architects Giuseppe Chigiotti, Ettore Sottsass, Marco Zanini,
Elio Di Franco, and to my dear friends Isa Vercelloni, Cinzia Mon-
cada and Lilli Bacci. Last but not least, I would like to thank Dr.
Angelika Taschen, the editor, Ursula Fethke, her assistant, Marion
Hauff, the art director, and Benedikt Taschen, the publisher of this
book, for their invaluable collaboration.

Paolo Rinaldi